Y0-BDB-321

The World's Most Spectacular
REPTILES & AMPHIBIANS

Text by
William W. Lamar

Photographs by
Pete Carmichael and Gail Shumway

Front Cover

The Javan Forest Dragon, *Gonocephalus chamaeleontinus*, is not only beautifully colored, but also bears elaborate ornamentation (see page 87). Photo by Gail Shumway.

Back Cover

The Philippine Pitviper, *Trimeresurus flavomaculatus flavomaculatus*, is found throughout the more than 7,000 islands of the Philippines, but exists nowhere else. It is one of the most colorful snakes in the world (see page 98). Photo by William W. Lamar

End Paper

A close-up photograph showing the lateral scales and colors of a Panther Chameleon (*Furcifer pardalis*). Chameleons are renowned for their ability to change colors according to their moods and social interactions (see page 38). Photo by Pete Carmichael.

Page One (Title Page)

The Painted Mantella, *Mantella madagascariensis*, resides in the rainforests of eastern Madagascar. Mantellas are similar to some of the Poison Frogs of Central and South America. Colors are a reliable way to identify Mantellas because they vary less than those of Poison Frogs. (see page 197). Photo by Gail Shumway.

Common Names of Reptiles and Amphibians

Each creature has a unique scientific name, its genus followed by its species, and sometimes also a subspecies. While scientists may argue about classification, the sytem is orderly. However, with common names, utter chaos reigns. Most common reptiles and amphibians are known by several or more names. Unlike the birds, whose common names have been standardized by an international committee over many years, the common names of reptiles and amphibians enjoy no such consensus. Consider a well-known snake in the US such as the Canebrake Rattlesnake, *Crotalus horridus atricaudatus*. Depending upon locality or the informant, this snake might legitimately be called any of the following names: Canebraker, Cane Rattler, Chevron Rattler, Common Timber Rattler, Rattlesnake of the Bottomlands, Seminole Rattler, Swamp Rattler, Southern-banded Rattlesnake, or Velvet-tailed Rattler. The situation is even worse for creatures whose range extends across national boundaries. In this book, the author has tried to follow established norms, and where none exist, to coin common names that are brief, yet as meaningful as possible.

The World's Most Spectacular Reptiles & Amphibians

Author: William W. Lamar
Photographers: Pete Carmichael and Gail Shumway
Editors: Winston Williams and Tim Ohr
Contributing Author: Bill Love

© 1997 by World Publications
First Edition
Library of Congresss No. 96-060955
ISBN: 1-884942-06-7
Manufactured in Malaysia

Consultants:
Peter A. Meylan was helpful in the preparation of the list of creatures to be included in this book. He also provided a number of useful referrals. Various other scientists, photographers, and individuals too numerous to mention, were helpful in locating specimens for photographs. Their contributions are appreciated.

Author's Acknowledgements:
Jonathan A. Campbell, Jerry Marzec, and Louis Porras courteously answered numerous questions. Nancy Fagan Lamar and Claire Simonds Lamar graciously tolerated my extensive absences while writing... a special thanks to them.

Photo Credits:
Dick Bartlett (DB), Pete Carmichael (PC), Dánte Fenolio (DF), Patricia and Michael Fogden (PMF), Paul Freed (PF), Carol Generoso (CG), John Iverson (JIV), Brian Kenney (BK), William W. Lamar (WL), David Liebman (DL), Bill Love (BL), Stan Osolinski (SO), Robert Pelham (RP), Louis Porras (LP), Peter C. H. Pritchard (PP), Dennis Sheridan (DS), Gail Shumway (GS), Paula Skoog (PS), Karl Switak(KS), and Bill Williamson (BW). Photo Agencies: José Azel/Aurora, Robin Cole/Eco-Stock, Damon Salceies/Eco-Stock, and Stephen Dalton/NHPA.

Other Titles Now Available in this Series:
The World's Most Beautiful
- *SEASHELLS*

New Titles Coming Soon:
The World's Most Spectacular
- *GEMS AND MINERALS*
- *BIRDS*
- *INSECTS*

World Publications
P.O. Box 24339
Tampa, Florida 33623 USA
Phone: 813-620-4517
Fax: 813-620-9096

CONTENTS

FOREWORD

$\mathcal{H}$ave you been looking for an inexpensive overview of the most colorful reptiles and amphibians? Look no further. Here is a superb collection of more than 400 beautiful color photographs, the work of highly acclaimed nature photographers. How exciting it is to see so many gems from their artistry.

William W. Lamar, author of this book, is not only an ace herpetologist, but also a talented photographer. He has spent years exploring South America, especially the vast *selva*, the jungles of the Amazon Basin, and portraying its biological treasures. Also, he has had access to captive collections, largely ones he assembled himself, which include creatures from almost every part of the globe.

Many of the pictures in this book were taken under field conditions, showing the animals in their natural habitats. Others are from captive specimens. All have been selected with care to provide a well-rounded sampling of the herpetological fauna from all over the globe.

How wonderful it would have been for me if this book had existed many years ago when I was struggling to become an efficient curator of reptiles at two different zoos, first at Toledo and then in Philadelphia. It would have opened a new world for me, helped me in choosing additions for our exhibits, and saved me endless hours digging out information from books and pamphlets.

Roger Conant
Author of *A Field Guide to the Reptiles and Amphibians of Eastern and Central North America* in the Peterson Field Guide series.

INTRODUCTION

This book was originally titled the world's most "beautiful" reptiles and amphibians, a selection of creatures appealing to the eyes of the publisher and photographers. "Beautiful," however, excluded many amazing creatures whose looks are strange and bizarre. It also excluded some animals rarely seen by science. It was decided, twelve months into the project, to broaden the scope of the book to include some of the most "spectacular" reptiles and amphibians in addition to the ones that could be considered beautiful.

There was another surprising reason for discarding the word "beautiful" from the title. It is a commentary on how even well-educated humans misunderstand these wonderful creatures. The title "beautiful" was opposed by some within the book industry who felt reptiles and amphibians could not be considered "beautiful." It is unfortunate that some people cannot see the beauty in these animals, but instead see them as "ugly" and "disgusting." Such an attitude often contributes to the persecution of certain species, some of which are endangered, and many whose populations are dwindling.

The selection process for this book, when the only criterion was "beauty," quickly provided hundreds of creatures. Once the criterion became "spectacular," the numbers under consideration jumped to thousands. Even the most plain and drab of species may exhibit individuals that vary in color or characteristics which are too spectacular to ignore. The publisher of this book has attempted to skim the finest cream to produce a "global celebration of reptiles and amphibians."

Unfortunately, many reptiles and amphibians world-wide are under attack. Most dangerous to their existence is the development and use of land by expanding human populations. Reptile and amphibian populations are also depleted by the pet trade, for their skins to become items of apparel, and sometimes through persecution when they are aimlessly slaughtered for "sport" or due to unjustified fear. In some rattlesnake "round-ups," the snakes are skinned alive because it is believed that their skins are more colorful when harvested this way. Conservation efforts, education, and captive breeding may be slowing down the decline or loss of these spectacular creatures, but much, much more needs to be done.

Humans are rapacious animals. They have reduced mighty bison herds to a few specimens, most often seen at a fair or in some form of exhibit. Man has severely depleted the whale populations of the earth's great oceans. Humans, through their industries, have altered the atmosphere, changed the amount of ultra-violet light reaching the earth, and polluted vast areas of water and land. Unless things change, more and more reptiles and amphibians will be seen only in photographs, and all the earth will be poorer for it. It is not only in the remote rainforests that these creatures are under assault. Some of the endangered creatures included here, such as the beautifully striped San Francisco Garter Snake, are from the Northern Hemisphere. It is hoped that this book, in a small way, will help humans everywhere appreciate and preserve these wonderful creatures.

The Editors

THE LIVING REPTILES

*R*eptiles first appeared on the earth about 315 million years ago, having apparently arisen from an amphibian ancestor. They share unique anatomical traits, including special modifications of their skin and eyes, the skull and backbone, and an external nasal gland. Over 6500 species are distributed world-wide on all continents except Antarctica. Due, in part, to their minimal food requirements, reptiles occupy nearly every kind of habitat imaginable, including the world's oceans, deserts, and montane (mountainous) regions as high as 16,500 feet above sea-level. Most reptiles are ectotherms, maintaining appropriate body temperatures by basking in optimal conditions, although some hormonal and muscular systems are involved in heat production in some species. During inclement seasons, reptiles can suspend many functions and remain dormant. There is considerable size variation within reptiles: tiny geckos (*Lepidoblepharis*) and chameleons (*Brookesia*) measure less than one inch in length; Komodo Monitors reach ten feet; Anacondas and Reticulated Pythons may be 25 feet or more; Leatherback Turtles and Indopacific Crocodiles have weights approaching one ton.

This diverse group of animals has influenced humans throughout recorded history. Objects of both revulsion and veneration since ancient times, reptiles figure strongly in myth and folklore. They have gained great popularity recently as the burgeoning field of herpetology reveals their interesting lifestyles. Ranging from the bizarre to the starkly beautiful, reptiles present a panorama of shapes and colors.

Modern reptiles encompass two venerable lineages: one includes the turtles and tortoises, while the other includes lizards, snakes, worm lizards, tuataras, and crocodilians. Recent evidence indicates that, tradition notwithstanding, the Reptilia cannot be separated reliably from the birds, with whom they have many shared traits. Doubtless, future scientific analyses will lead to changes in the way reptiles and birds are grouped.

Typical reptiles possess dry skin covered with scales. Snakes also have a brille, or protective eye covering. Like other animals, reptiles shed their skins, but they do so at one time rather than continually. They may be limbless or nearly so, and some lizards, and some worm lizards, possess only one pair of limbs. Limbless terrestrial reptiles move via some form of undulation. Those with limbs crawl, while some lizard species rear up, using only the hind limbs, when running fast.

Fertilization is internal, and in most reptile species there are sexual differences in size or color. Males of some species of lizard attain remarkable colors during breeding season. Certain lizard populations consist entirely of females, each genetic duplicates of the other. One island population of snakes is entirely hermaphroditic, with all individuals possessing both male and female characteristics. The majority of reptiles produce leathery-shelled eggs which, in contrast to amphibian eggs, are resistant to drying.

Crocodilians and most turtles construct nests of vegetation or excavate burrows for their eggs. All other reptiles deposit their eggs in humus, on the forest floor, or adhered to bark or something similar. Many kinds of snakes and lizards display some type of viviparity, producing live young. Parental care is largely absent in reptiles, with offspring quite capable of subsisting on their own from birth. However, some lizard and snake species brood their eggs, and egg-brooding and parental care in crocodilians is widely documented. In some species of turtles and crocodilians, the sex of the offspring is determined by the temperature during incubation.

Reptiles are preyed upon by a variety of organisms including humans, other reptiles, amphibians, birds, mammals, fishes, and many kinds of invertebrates. Some of their defense mechanisms involve camouflage (direct resemblance to something in the environment), cryptic or disruptive coloration (rendering the animal difficult to see), mimicry (resembling something noxious), a wide array of threat displays (including puffing, flattening, gaping, and hissing), death feigning, fleeing the scene (even via gliding), biting, scratching, and lashing or breaking the tail.

Although most of the negative image of reptiles is unfounded, some species are capable of causing suffering or death in humans. Several species of crocodilians have preyed on humans, sometimes in considerable numbers, especially in Africa and Indonesia. There are many dangerously venomous species of snakes throughout the world, and even the venomous Gila Monster (*Heloderma*) and the large Komodo Monitor *(Varanus)* have caused human fatalities. Thus, it is not surprising that reptiles have been the object of considerable toxicological and behavioral research. This has led to greater understanding and management of wild populations (and humans) as well as important breakthroughs in the areas of medicine and snake venom research.

Reptiles are exploited for the leather industry, as food sources, for the pet industry, and for medicinal purposes. Due to these factors, and especially because of environmental destruction, many species are endangered to some degree. Promotion of alternative materials can help reduce the demand for reptile hides. Captive breeding already is reducing the drain on wild populations. Perhaps with increased conservation education, pressure to protect critical habitats can be heightened. This is especially necessary in the tropics where reptiles reach their greatest diversity and where indiscriminate land use is most damaging.

TURTLES AND TORTOISES

Turtles are among the world's most distinctive animals due to their "suit of armor," the bony shell in which they live. There are nearly 250 living species of turtles (and tortoises) recognized today. They are distributed throughout the world on every continent except Antartica, and in every ocean. They occupy freshwater and marine habitats, deserts, tropical and temperate forests, and mountain regions.

The smallest turtles, like the Speckled Cape Tortoise (*Homopus signatus*) scarcely span four inches in length, while at the opposite end of the spectrum there are giants like the Leatherback (*Dermochelys coriacea*), at over 2,000 pounds, the world's heaviest reptile. Some tortoises can weigh in excess of 550 pounds. Many seaturtles, the gargantuan Alligator Snapping Turtle (*Macroclemmys temminckii*), the Amazon River Turtle (*Podocnemis expansa*), and the Narrow-Headed Softshell Turtle (*Chitra indica*) can reach weights of two to five hundred pounds or more.

While some species have reduced or flexible shells, turtles are still instantly recognizable. In fact, shelled turtles are an ancient lineage. They have walked the earth for at least 200 million years. Because of the restrictions caused by the shell, the pectoral and pelvic portions of the turtle skeleton lie within the rib cage, a situation unique among vertebrates. In addition to the distinctive shell, the skull of turtles is unique among reptiles because it lacks openings in the cheek region. There is little difference between the sexes in most species, except for certain aspects of shell size.

Fertilization is internal, and eggs are deposited in burrows, rotting vegetation, or sometimes on the forest floor. Incubation in some species is lengthy (several months), and the sex of the offspring is temperature-dependent in a few turtles.

Some highly aquatic species are capable of absorbing oxygen through the skin or through special sacks in the tail region, but all turtles possess and use lungs. Famed for their slow gait, some species of turtles are capable of short bursts of speed. Many aquatic species can swim quite rapidly and gracefully.

Many kinds of turtles feed on vegetable matter, and some specialize in eating mollusks, jellyfish, or similiar items. However, most turtles are opportunists, and they will accept a wide array of dietary items including invertebrates, small vertebrates, fruits, plants, and carrion. While many turtles simply graze on sedentary or immobile food objects, some are ambush feeders. Others possess special appendages which serve as active or passive lures to attract prey within reach.

There are two categories of turtles: those that withdraw the neck vertically (nine or eleven families, depending on the authority) and those that withdraw the neck horizontally (two families). The first category includes seaturtles, famed for their migrations across the oceans and for their spectacular nesting aggregations on warm beaches. Also in this group are the Snapping Turtles of the Western Hemisphere, the spectacular and endangered Central American River Turtle (*Dermatemys mawii*) and its relatives: the Musk, Pig-nosed, and Softshell Turtles. The last group of turtles that vertically withdraw the neck might well be termed typical turtles, as they include the familiar Box, Pond, and River Turtles primarily of temperate regions, and the terrestrial tortoises.

The two turtle families of the second category are found in freshwater habitats in the Southern Hemisphere. They include most of the inland species found in Africa and South America. They are the only non-marine turtles occurring on Australia and New Guinea. Members include the highly aquatic Fitzroy River Turtle (*Rheodytes leukops*) of Australia, and perhaps the world's most bizarre turtle, the Matamata (*Chelus fimbriatus*). Another member is the critically endangered Western Swamp Turtle (*Pseudemydura umbrina*) whose entire distribution only encompasses 530 acres. The spectacular sideneck turtles of the Amazon and Orinoco Basins, now seriously depleted by indiscriminant egg-harvesting, also form part of this group.

Long famed for their purported slowness, and for longevity (150 years or more for some), turtles are perhaps the one group of reptiles humans do not revile. They have been kept as pets, eaten, and their shells admired and used for many purposes. Seaturtles, those restless wanderers of the high seas, have captured the public's imagination with their romantic and prodigal migrations and spectacular nesting rituals. They are endangered because of unscrupulous over-harvesting. Their plight echoes that faced by most turtles as the world's great wild places rapidly disappear. One can only hope that these worthy symbols of conservation will galvanize humans into moderation so that turtles can continue to be a part of our future.

Northern Diamondback Terrapin
Malaclemys terrapin terrapin

A denizen of brackish water, this Map Turtle relative can be found along quiet coastal marshes and estuaries in the eastern US and Gulf of Mexico. Seven races are recognized, each differing slightly in aspects of color and pattern. Diamondback Terrapins feed primarily upon mollusks, crustaceans, and fish. For many years this species was over-harvested. Happily, it has made a comeback, although it is still prized among gourmets.

Peninsula Cooter (hatchling)
Pseudemys
floridana peninsularis

It is common to see several dozen of these ten- to sixteen-inch turtles during warm weather, as they pile themselves onto suitable basking logs. Native to peninsular Florida, in the southeastern part of the US, these gregarious reptiles are especially at-home in large, slow rivers, lakes and large ponds. Active by day, they hunt for aquatic vegetation, their primary diet. Because of their habit of wandering about on land, many cooters are struck by automobiles.

Western Painted Turtle *Chrysemys picta bellii*

Largest of the painted turtles at over nine inches, this attractive species is found in the American midwest and adjacent Canada. Sporting delicate red and yellow lines on a greenish to black skin, this reptile is a familiar site as it basks on logs in ponds and lakes. Males court the larger females by gently vibrating their elongated claws along the sides of the female's head while the turtles face each other.

Florida Redbelly Turtle

Pseudemys nelsoni

Native to Florida and southeast Georgia in the US, this 12-inch turtle occupies streams, marshes, bayous, lakes, and even the coastal mangrove zone. These reptiles are conspicuous as they bask on logs in the sun. Both hatchling and young Florida Redbelly Turtles are carnivorous, consuming a variety of insect and animal matter, while adults are primarily herbivorous, feeding upon aquatic vegetation.

10

Red-eared Slider *Trachemys scripta elegans*

Originally found in the central US and adjacent northeast Mexico, this turtle's distribution today is far more complicated. Its attractiveness and hardy nature caused the Red-ear to be exploited heavily for the pet trade. In fact, the demand grew to such a point that turtle farms were established, producing millions of babies that were shipped—and often released—around the world. Many of these introductions were successful, and now there are Red-eared Sliders occurring in many parts of the world. They can even be found in South Africa and Singapore, where captives escaped and established populations.

The foot-long females, because they must produce and contain eggs, are much larger than the males. Adult males use their long nails to stroke the females' facial region during courtship. The common name derives from the distinctive and showy red patch on the sides of the head. These patches are unique among North American turtles. Red-ears feed on a wide variety of plant and animal material, and this perhaps has aided them in colonizing areas into which they have been released. Juveniles tend to be carnivorous, but adults feed heavily on plant matter.

As with any animal, inherited pigment defects can produce unusual patterns. The albino specimens shown at left lack the green color typical of normal Red-ears.

Alligator Snapping Turtle

Macroclemys temminckii

With a shell length of over two feet and a weight of over 300 pounds, this denizen of rivers and bayous of the southeastern US qualifies as one of the world's largest turtles. Surprisingly active and alert, this impressive reptile is a forager, feeding primarily on acorns and mussels. It is also a fisherman, using a worm-like lure in its gaping mouth to entice turtles and fishes to within striking range. Dwindling in numbers throughout its range due to harvesting for the food market, this inoffensive creature is finally receiving protection in some states.

The photo at right shows the red tongue-like lure of a young Alligator Snapper.

12

Indian Roofed Turtle *Kachuga tecta*

This nine-inch turtle, also called the Indian Tent Turtle, favors quiet waters and lives in ponds, streams, and oxbow lakes from Pakistan east across northern and peninsular India to Bangladesh. Strangely, this very familiar species is practically unstudied. Almost nothing is known of its natural history. It is primarily herbivorous and is a rather poor swimmer. Habitat destruction and other threats have placed this turtle under government protection. Nothing has been reported about incubation time, nest sites, or clutch sizes for this species.

Yellow-blotched Map Turtle

Graptemys flavimaculata

This elegant aquatic reptile is restricted to the drainage system of the Pascagoula and Chickasawhay rivers in southern Mississippi, US. "Sawbacks," as Map Turtles are sometimes called, are fond of basking, and they are a common and typical sight of the region as they lay, piled one upon the other, on tree trunks and limbs near the water's edge. Unlike sliders and cooters, which prefer quiet waters, Sawbacks are adapted for life in deep, fast-flowing streams. A small species that does not exceed seven inches in length, this turtle feeds pre-dominantly on aquatic insects and perhaps mollusks. Sawbacks bear a strong superficial similarity to the Roofed Turtles of Asia (shown above).

ECO-STOCK/DAMON SALCEIES

Box Turtles

Some turtle species are capable of closing their shells in order to hide from predators. They are found primarily in North America and in Southeast Asia. Collectively, they are called Box Turtles, although some forms are not closely related. American Box Turtles often amble across backyards and roads making them among the most familiar of all US reptiles. Found over much of the south-central US and parts of adjacent Mexico, these turtles are often picked up and kept as pets by children. Well protected by their completely closeable shell, Box Turtles are famed for their longevity. Based on dated carvings in their shells, some specimens are believed to have surpassed the century mark. In the southeastern US, Box Turtles are being decimated by the introduced Fire Ant (*Solenopsis invicta*).

Mexican Box Turtle *Terrapene carolina mexicana*

Most North American Box Turtles with bright red irises are males. Females tend to have brown eyes. This race of the Eastern Box Turtle occurs in northeastern Mexico.

BL

BK

Florida Box Turtle *Terrapene carolina bauri*

Often seen crossing highways, this attractive reptile is the southeastern race of the Eastern Box Turtle. It occurs in peninsular Florida as far south as the Keys. Moist woodland and pine flatwoods are its preferrred habitat. This turtle faces habitat reduction due to extensive development.

Eastern Box Turtle *Terrapene carolina carolina*

The Eastern Box Turtle is an inhabitant of fields, woodland, and pastures in the US. Box Turtles feed on a variety of insects and vegetable matter and are regular visitors to neighborhood yards, often to the delight of children. Due to their slow gait, Box Turtles are vulnerable to lawn mowers and automobiles.

Chinese Yellow-margined Box Turtle
Cistoclemmys flavomarginata sinensis

As the common name implies, these six-inch turtles can completely close their shell, and thus retreat from enemies. A native of ponds and rice paddies in southern China, this species forages by day for plants, insects, and perhaps carrion. Although it is semi-aquatic, the Yellow-margined Box Turtle spends much of its time on land. By no means a rare species, its natural history remains unstudied.

Ornate Box Turtle *Terrapene ornata ornata*

The six-inch Ornate Box Turtle is native to portions of Texas and midwestern US. It prowls by day in search of insects and small vertebrates, upon which it preys with surprising agility. Like most other box turtles, this species frequently falls victim to automobiles as it attempts to cross roadways while foraging.

Indochinese Box Turtle *Cuora galbinifrons galbinifrons*

A shy denizen of shrubby, upland forests, this eight-inch turtle is primarily a carnivore, feeding on earthworms and similar items. Native to Vietnam, southern Guangxi Province and Hainan Island in China, this is the least aquatic member of its genus. It is most common at intermediate to high elevations.

15

Wood Turtle (North American) *Clemmys insculpta*

Conspicuous because of tree-like growth rings that etch its shell (hence, the name "Wood Turtle"), this reptile displays a degree of intelligence and curiosity seldom obvious among its relatives. Some populations have mastered the art of stomping on the ground to induce earthworms to come to the surface (perhaps seeking to evade a mole) where the turtles capture them. Wood Turtles interact within a complex social hierarchy and feature a number of ritualized behaviors. Native to the northeastern US and adjacent Canada, this 12-inch terrestrial reptile lives in close association with water. It feeds on insects, amphibians, and plant matter.

This view shows the sculpted three-dimensional pattern which gives this turtle its common name. Wood turtles are adept climbers, and are capable of scrambling over many difficult obstacles.

Spotted Turtle *Clemmys guttata*

This five-inch, shy cousin of the Wood Turtle ranges from Ontario, Canada, and Maine, southward to Florida. It is at home equally on land or in water. Favored haunts include small woodland streams, bogs, and wet pastures. After spring mating, females construct nests in soft soil. Cool temperatures are preferred, and this species will retreat from high summer heat by hiding in muskrat lodges or similar locales.

Spiny Turtle *Heosemys spinosa*

A triumph of design, the turtle shell has undergone little modification since its first appearance many millions of years ago. Still, some species manage to be unique, and the Spiny Turtle, with a series of spikes around the periphery of its shell, is certainly one of these. Spiny Turtles can be found as they walk through shallow creeks eating plant and animal matter in rainforests from Myanmar (Burma) and Thailand to Malaysia and Indonesia. Presumably, predators would find the spiny shell unappetizing, although the six-to-eight-inch adults have worn away most of the spikes. Females lay a single, large, elongate egg, which is hidden among vegetation on the ground.

Tropical Wood Turtle *Rhinoclemmys pulcherrima manni*

The four races of this attractive turtle are distributed from Mexico through Central America. They are semi-aquatic and are found in marshy lowland forest, savanna, or gallery forest. Most varieties are omnivorous. The race shown here is found in lowland forests of Nicaragua and Costa Rica. Unlike most turtles, Tropical Wood Turtles are poor nest-builders that do not bury their eggs.

Black-breasted Leaf Turtle *Geoemyda spengleri*

This five-inch turtle is a forest-dweller that ranges from southern China to Vietnam. Occasionally, it walks through small streams while foraging for food. Its lifestyle is transitional between that of a typical aquatic turtle and that of a terrestrial species. Basking is accomplished in small, sunny places on the forest floor. Due to their habit of staring inquisitively, these turtles give the impression of being unusually intelligent.

Mata Mata *Chelus fimbriatus*

Undoubtedly this is the world's weirdest-looking turtle, with its snorkle nose, leering grin, and leaf-like skin flaps covering the head and neck. Blending beautifully with its surroundings at river bottom, this fish-eater "vacuums" its unwary prey by suddenly opening its mouth and inhaling the fish into its roomy throat. The fish is swallowed whole and the excess water is expelled. Weighing as much as 38 pounds, this reptile is found in the lowlands of the Amazon and Orinoco river basins.

Red Toad-headed Turtle

Phrynops rufipes

Bedecked in brilliant red, a color unusual for a turtle, this shy denizen of rainforest streams makes its home in the Rio Negro system of Brazil and Colombia. Seldom seen because of secretive habits and the secluded areas it occupies, this ten-inch turtle forages actively along the streambed for insects and small fishes. Its shell is used as a musical instrument by some Tukanoan tribes.

Introduction to Side-necked Turtles

There are two families of turtles that withdraw their necks laterally. The neck is folded to the side in order to protect it beneath the shell, rather than withdrawing the head directly, as is typical for most turtles. Today, their representatives can be found in South America, Africa, Madagascar, the Seychelles Islands, and the Indo-Australian Archipelago. These are turtles of tropical inland waters, and they range in size from the massive Amazon Sideneck, or Arrau, *Podocnemis expansa*, to the diminutive Western Swamp Turtle, *Pseudemydura umbrina*, one of the most endangered animals in the world.

Reimann's Snakeneck Turtle (left)
Chelodina reimanni

There are relatively few turtle species in the world, so it is unusual to encounter one not known to science. Reimann's Snakeneck Turtle, however, was first described in 1990. Perhaps this reptile was only recently discovered because it lives in remote rivers in southeastern Irian Jaya, Indonesia, and extreme southwestern Papua, New Guinea. Like most snakenecks, this twelve-inch turtle is highly aquatic and feeds on a variety of invertebrates and fishes.

Black-backed Twistneck Turtle (below)
Platemys platycephala melanonota

One of the Amazon Basin's beautiful turtles, this seven-inch reptile makes its home in and along clear-water streams running through white-sand forest. It occurs in Ecuador and Peru. The Twistneck Turtle is a poor swimmer and prefers to walk through shallow pools in quest of insects, fruits, and small vertebrates upon which it feeds.

Leopard Tortoise *Geochelone pardalis*

Unlike its namesake, this 30-inch tortoise is not a carnivore. The similarity pertains to the leopard-like spots which adorn the impressive, high-domed shell of the adult. This pattern may render the turtle difficult to detect in dappled sunlight. (The photo at top shows a young tortoise. The large markings will turn to speckles with maturity as shown in the photo above.) It is found in savanna and open woodland from Sudan and Angola to the Republic of South Africa.

Introduction to Tortoises

There are about 50 living species in the family Testudinidae, popularly called tortoises. Tortoises are terrestrial, although many are fond of water and enter it freely. They range in size from gigantic Galapagos and Aldabra tortoises, which may exceed 500 pounds, to tiny Cape Tortoises, mature at four inches.

Indian Star Tortoise *Geochelone elegans*

Occupying tropical deciduous forests and dry savannas, this 11-inch tortoise requires a good water supply. Ranging from Pakistan through India and Sri Lanka to Bangladesh and possibly Myanmar (Burma), this attractive turtle is mostly herbivorous, foraging for grasses, flowers, fruits, and sometimes carrion. Like many tortoise species, males utter grunting sounds during mating. Three to ten eggs are laid and buried, taking as much as five months to develop. Specimens from the northern portions of the range tend to be larger, although the insular population on Sri Lanka includes some of the biggest specimens.

Radiated Tortoise

Geochelone (Astrochelys) radiata

This beautiful tortoise is a native of southern Madagascar. It has been introduced on Mauritius and Reunion island and inhabits arid thorn forests. Export of this turtle is strictly controlled by Madagascar because it is threatened by human encroachment and predation. One specimen is known to have survived 137 years in captivity, one of the longest lifespans of any turtle. This high-domed sixteen-inch herbivore lays up to 12 eggs.

Flat-shelled Spider Tortoise

Pyxis (Acinixys) planicauda

Tiny, at only five to six inches, and limited to two dry forests in its native western Madagascar, this tortoise leads a secretive life. Remaining hidden in leaf litter during the dry season, Spider Tortoises become active when the rains begin. After breeding, females deposit a single egg. Cutting of forest poses a serious threat to the future of this timid reptile.

Galápagos Tortoise *Geochelone (Chelonoidis) nigra ssp.*

Considered by various authorities to represent either twelve species or twelve races of a single species, these gigantic turtles live in the Galápagos Archipelago off the coast of Ecuador. The complex includes the largest living tortoises, with a shell length of up to four feet and weights in excess of 500 pounds. Like most island creatures, these turtles lead a precarious existence. Rampaging rat, domestic cat, and goat populations, all introduced by humans, upset the delicate balance of life in the Galápagos. Historically, these giant reptiles were harvested as meat for sailors. If unmolested, the Galápagos Tortoise can live for more than 100 years. The photo at top shows the tortoises on the slopes of the Alcedo Volcano. Above, a Galápagos Tortoise interacts with a visitor at the Darwin Station research facility.

Red-footed Tortoise

Geochelone (Chelonoidis) carbonaria

A terrestrial denizen of coastal dry forest and inland savannas, this 15-inch tortoise ranges from Panama and Colombia south to Paraguay in South America. Absent from rainforests, this turtle forages actively for all manner of plant and animal matter on which it feeds. Like its relative, the Yellow-footed Tortoise, this reptile will feed on carrion when the opportunity presents itself. Eggs are deposited in burrows in the ground.

Where in the World to Find Tortoises

Tropical tortoises, the majority of the family, are represented in Africa, Madagascar, Aldabra and the Seychelles, India, Southeast Asia, and South America (including the Galapagos Archipelago). There also are tortoises in southern North America, Europe, and adjacent West Asia.

Western Tent Tortoise *Psammobates tentorius trimeni*

Easily one of the world's most beautiful turtles, the Western Tent Tortoise is most often seen as it wanders about after a rainstorm. Native to coastal sandy regions of Namaqualand, South Africa, this six-inch reptile browses during the early morning and late afternoon for the plant matter which makes up its diet.

African Spurred Tortoise

Geochelone (Centrochelys) sulcata

Only the gigantic tortoises from Aldabra and the Galapagos surpass the Spurred Tortoise in size. As much as 30 inches in length, these turtles occupy a belt of savannas extending across Africa from Senegal and Mauritania to Ethiopia, south of the Sahara Desert. Because its habitat is so seasonally dry, this species must depend on metabolic water and moisture derived from the plant matter on which it feeds. The Spurred Tortoise is active mostly at dawn and dusk, and it digs long burrows to avoid the midday heat.

Parrot-beaked Tortoise *Homopus areolatus*

This four-inch turtle makes its home in moist coastal heathlands and thornveld in the Cape Province of South Africa. Timid, these tortoises forage near brushy shelter, and frequently hide beneath rocks or in burrows. Females produce two to three eggs which may require up to ten months to develop. Adept climbers, these reptiles search for just about any kind of plant or animal matter as food. This species is known to have a life span of at least 28 years.

Geometric Tortoise

Psammobates geometricus

This seven-inch tortoise is found only in the southwestern Cape Province, Republic of South Africa. Its habitat, coastal flatlands, has been altered extensively due to agricultural pressures, and today this ranks as one of the world's rarest turtles. In fact, it is so uncommon that its natural history remains largely an enigma. These tortoises are active during winter and early spring, with nesting during September and October. Eggs require up to 210 days to develop.

Angonoka

Geochelone (Astrochelys) yniphora

Restricted to a 39-square-mile area in northwestern Madagascar, this beautiful tortoise is one of the rarest, and perhaps the most endangered of all tortoises in the world. Aside from habitat encroachment, feral pigs pose a grave threat to this turtle's future. Intensive captive breeding efforts are currently underway and it is hoped that the species can be reproduced in sufficient numbers to ensure its survival. Maximum size is nearly 18 inches. Its diet consists of legumes and grasses.

Florida Softshell Turtle *Apalone ferox* (above)

This two-foot turtle can be found in all freshwater habitats in the Southeastern US. The long, tubular nostrils serve a function. They act as snorkels, allowing the Softshell to breathe by just extending the tips above the water surface, so as to not attract any attention.

Narrow-headed Softshell Turtle (left)

Chitra indica

Nearly four feet wide as a large adult, this softshell turtle is so heavy it can only walk with difficulty. However, it is swift and graceful in the water. Its range is from Pakistan, India, Nepal, and Bangladesh through Myanmar (Burma) to western Thailand and northern Malaysia. This turtle lives in sandy bends of large rivers, where it pursues fish and a variety of invertebrates. Females deposit their eggs in a nest on land.

Leatherback Turtle
Dermochelys coriacea

One of the largest living reptiles, surpassed in size only by some crocodiles, Leatherbacks have exceeded eight feet in length and weighed over 2,000 pounds, although these specimens are exceptional. Because of their thick and oily dermis (as oppposed to the traditional shell), Leatherbacks can exploit colder waters than other seaturtles. They have been found off of Newfoundland and Labrador in the north, and Mar del Plata, Argentina, in the south. Their range is worldwide, the largest of any reptile, and includes both temperate and tropical oceans. Deep-diving denizens of the open seas, adults feed primarily on jellyfish. From 46 to 160 eggs are laid on beachs at night, usually from January through March, the nesting season. Powerful, but normally inoffen-sive, on occasion this turtle may capsize small fishing boats, perhaps mistaking them for other Leatherbacks.

Many people think that seaturtles are crying when they observe the copious flow of liquid from the nesting turtle's eyes. Fortunately, this is not the case. Seaturtles possess salt glands, with openings located at the base of the eyes. These glands flow constantly, even while the turtle is in the water, and they aid the reptile in controlling the level of salt in its body. The solution excreted is highly concentrated with salt, thus helping the kidneys to function. While ashore, the moisture includes mucous which undoubtedly aids in washing sand from the turtle's eyes.

These ancient creatures (the crocodiles, alligators, caimans and gharials) are the largest and most awe-inspiring of the world's reptiles. Crocodilians have been around for at least 240 million years, and three lineages, long separated one from the other, exist today. Although there are not very many species in this group (only 22), there remains considerable uncertainty about relationships. Some authorities partition the crocodilians into three families while others lump them together in one family.

Like all other reptiles, with the exception of turtles, crocodilians possess skulls with two openings in the cheek region on either side. Apart from their distinctive shape and scalation, crocodilians share some unique features, including a four-chambered heart and a brain which is more advanced than that of any other reptile. In many ways, these creatures are most similar to the birds, which arose from the same group of Archosaurs (Ruling Reptiles) that gave rise to the crocodilians.

Because of their semi-aquatic lifestyle, crocodilians possess many modifications that aid in swimming, hunting, and eating in the water. These include valvular ears and nostrils, a special protective membrane covering the eye, acute hearing, elevated eyes and nostrils, and a valvular throat. Basking provides a critical means of temperature regulation.

Fertilization is internal and all species lay eggs which are deposited in nests constructed of decaying vegetation. Parental care is complex, and most species at least guard the nest during incubation.

In addition to humans, crocodilians are preyed on by mammals, fishes, birds, and reptiles. Although adept at hiding or remaining motionless, these reptiles can defend themselves with their powerful jaws if cornered.

Crocodilians are carnivores. Some species are specialized predators of fishes, but most are opportunistic, eating anything they can capture. Many varieties undergo dietary shifts with age, feeding as juveniles on crustaceans and other invertebrates, then fishes, and finally large mammals as adults. Several species have historically been implicated in human fatalities. The Nile Crocodile (Crocodylus Niloticus) has been responsible for more deaths in Africa than all other kinds of wildlife. Of course, this pales when compared with the massive slaughter of crocodilians engendered by the leather industry.

Alligators and Caimans are found from southeastern North America through Central and South America, with one species, the Chinese Alligator (*Alligator sinensis*) occurring in eastern China. Ranging in size from the five-foot Dwarf Caiman (*Paleosuchus palpebrosus*) to the Black Caiman (*Caiman niger*) which can exceed 18 feet in length, this group is distinguished by the socket in the skull into which the fourth madibular tooth inserts when the mouth is closed.

Gharials (*Gavialis gangeticus*) are huge, slender-snouted, fish-eaters which can reach 18 feet in length. They are found from Bangladesh across northern India and Nepal to Pakistan. The tip of the elongated snout is greatly swollen in males. Critically endangered, Gharials have responded positively to intensive breeding programs. Their relationship to the superficially similar False Gavial (*Tomistoma schlegelii*) is the subject of dispute, and the latter is included with the crocodiles by most authorities.

Crocodiles world-wide include fourteen species in three genera found in tropical and subtropical regions. One species, the Mugger (*Crocodylus palustris*), extends into temperate southern Asia. The smallest crocodile is the Congo Dwarf Crocodile (*Osteolaemis tetraspis osbornei*) at scarcely five feet. Some specimens of the genus *Crocodylus* have been known to exceed 20 feet in length, with weights approaching a ton. In true crocodiles, the large fourth madibular tooth is exposed when the jaws are closed. Some crocodiles are restricted to freshwater habitats while others are adapted to life in estuaries, sometimes even wandering far out to sea.

Indopacific (Salt Water) Crocodile

Crocodylus porosus

One of the largest, possibly the largest, of the living crocodilians, this imposing creature lives in estuaries, marshes, lakes, and large rivers from southwestern India and Sri Lanka to Indochina, the Philippines, the Australasian Archipelago, New Guinea, northern Australia, the Solomon and Caroline Islands, to Ponape. Maximum size is subject to dispute, as is always the case with large reptiles, but individuals of this species are known to reach over 20 feet in length and weigh as much as 2,200 pounds. Known for its lengthy travels in the ocean, this reptile has colonized many islands. It feeds on almost anything it can subdue, and throughout its range the Indopacific Crocodile has caused many human fatalities.

American Crocodile *Crocodylus acutus*

This imposing reptile can reach a length of 20 feet, although it is usually only half that size. A denizen of coastal rivers, lakes, and estuaries, this crocodile ranges from southern Florida in the US, through Cuba, the Cayman Islands, Jamaica, Hispaniola, Martinique, Trinidad, Margarita, and on the mainland from Mexico south to Colombia, coastal Ecuador and Peru. Hatchlings dine on insects and crustaceans, adding larger vertebrates as they attain maturity. This species is the only crocodile found in the US, and it is slowly increasing in numbers because of its protected status.

29

Morelet's Crocodile *Crocodylus moreletii*

With a distribution limited to southern Mexico, Belize, and Guatemala, this 10-foot crocodile is primarily an occupant of fresh water habitats. An important icon in early Mayan culture, today this reptile is greatly reduced in numbers. It lives primarily in the upper stretches of streams and rivers, as well as ponds, lakes, and marshes. Prey items include mollusks, fishes, and small mammals.

Cuban Crocodile *Crocodylus rhombifer*

Found only in Cuba's Zapata swamp and Isla de la Juventud, this is an unusually aggressive crocodile. Hunted for its colorful hide, this species has been decimated not only by hunters and habitat loss, but also because of captive interbreeding with the American Crocodile, and through competition with the introduced Spectacled Caiman. Unfortunately, farming operations in Cuba are presently breeding very few pure Cuban Crocodiles. One of the smaller species, the Cuban Crocodile reaches a maximum length of just under 12 feet. Its diet consists of fishes and mammals.

Nile Crocodile *Crocodylus niloticus*

At over 15 feet in length, possessed of enormous strength and speed, the Nile Crocodile has accounted for more human fatalities in its native Africa than any other predator on the continent. Important carnivores whose activities aid in maintaining their aquatic habitats for all wildlife, Nile Crocodiles are surprisingly tender parents. The female assists the calling hatchlings from their eggs by gently removing the shells, then carrying the babies to the water in her mouth. Nile Crocs feed on invertebrates, fishes, and small animals. Large adults will tackle prey as large as buffalo.

Black Caiman *Caiman niger*

Averaging 8 to 12 feet, Black Caimans have been measured at lengths in excess of 20 feet, making them one of the largest crocodilians in the western hemisphere. Native to the Amazon Basin and northeastern South America, this boldly marked species has been much persecuted by the hide industry. Today it is abundant nowhere, but it seems to be increasing in numbers, especially in oxbow lakes and isolated lagoons. Adults feed primarily on mammals and fishes. Males aggressively help to maintain their territories by vocalizing.

American Alligator

Alligator mississippiensis

A typical denizen of nearly any body of water in the southeast United States, this imposing creature averages six to twelve feet in length. Long persecuted for their valuable hides, alligators have made a spectacular comeback under strict protection. The brightly colored juveniles feed on insects and crustaceans. As they grow older, their colors dull and their diet changes to fish, turtles, and eventually mammals. Females construct a large mound of debris from vegetation and deposit up to four dozen eggs inside. The nest and hatchlings are zealously protected by the mother, who will respond aggressively to the grunting distress calls of the juveniles.

PMF

Gharial *Gavialis gangeticus*

One of the world's largest and heaviest crocodilians, the Gharial (sometimes called Gavial) ranges from Pakistan to Myanmar (Burma). It has a long, absurdly slender snout, an adaptation for capturing the fish which make up the Gharial's diet. Due to years of hunting and persecution for its hide, this creature is seldom seen in the wild. Captive breeding efforts in India have been successful in helping to save this magnificent creature from extinction. During the mating season, the males sport a ghara, or nose knob, a swelling at the tip of the snout. This functions as a resonator, increasing the sounds the animal makes. This presumably aids in territorial defense. The Gharial's common name derives from this distinctive swelling.

False Gharial

Tomistoma schlegelii

One of the few crocodilians retaining distinctive juvenile markings into adulthood, these slender-snouted and graceful beasts live in freshwater habitats from the Malaysian Peninsula south through part of Indonesia and possibly Sulawesi. Their lineage is ancient, dating to Eocene times. Up to thirteen feet in length, False Gharials feed primarily upon small vertebrates and fish.

PC

THE LEPIDOSAURIA

*L*epidosaurians, "scaly reptiles," include the Tuataras (*Sphenodon*), the Worm Lizards (*Amphisbaenians*), lizards, and snakes. There are two species of Tuataras, both confined to islands of New Zealand, where they live in burrows in sea-bird rookeries. Known to live up to 77 years in captivity, these "beak-heads" are superficially similar to lizards and considered by many authorities to be unrelated to all other extant (still existing) reptiles. The Worm Lizards are burrowing reptiles, either limbless or possessing a single pair of limbs, with reduced eyes, that are found world-wide except for Australia and the Orient. There are about 140 species grouped in 23 genera and 4 families; they are variously considered to be closely related to snakes or to lizards or to neither. Worm Lizards are found primarily in tropical and subtropical regions. The remaining lepidosaurs are the squamate reptiles (the lizards and snakes), which are herein treated separately.

LIZARDS

*W*ith over 3800 species and 22 families, the lizards are the most diverse of the reptiles. They are found all over the world except for Antartica and most of the area spanned by the Arctic Circle. Lizards exist on many oceanic islands, and they occupy habitats ranging from temperate forests and prairies to tropical rainforests, deserts, and seashores, extending from sea-level up to over 16,000 feet elevation. Some are adapted for a life in the trees, others live beneath the earth's surface, many live in and around water, and others even live under sand. The 22 families include a great diversity of shapes and sizes. There are snake-like lizards, limbless lizards, species with prehensile (grasping) tails, species adorned with fin-like structures....the variety seems endless. The world's smallest reptiles are tiny lizards (a gecko and a chameleon) but the largest member of the tribe is the imposing Komodo Monitor (*Varanus komodoensis*) which can reach ten feet and more than 300 pounds.

Lizards first appeared during the Triassic Period, about 230 million years ago. They share many unique skeletal characteristics. They are covered by scales, usually possess moveable eyelids, an external ear opening, a fused mandible, a well-developed tongue, and specialized teeth. With the exception of some unisexual populations, fertilization is internal, and either eggs are laid (in humus or burrows) or live young are born. Some species are seasonal breeders, and some species brood their eggs, although parental care is not a common occurrence among the lizards. Many lizard species are highly social, and elaborate courtship and territorial rituals are seen in species from all continents.

Lizards include carnivores (meat-eaters) and herbivores (plant-eaters). Most of the smaller species feed on invertebrates, while larger species eat everything from crabs to mammals, birds, reptiles, amphibians, and eggs. The various species of herbivores feed on flowers, leaves, cacti, algae, fruits and berries. In turn, many creatures feed on lizards, so they possess a variety of defense mechanisms including breakable and toxic tails, venomous bites (Gila Monster and Beaded Lizards), strong claws and teeth, camouflage and cryptic coloration.

Most specialists recognize three lineages of lizards. One includes the Geckos and Scaly-foots, with nearly 850 species in 93 genera and two or three families. These soft-skinned, large-eyed lizards are found worldwide, mostly in tropical to subtropical climes, but extending up to several thousand feet above sea-level. The Iguanians include the Chameleons and Agamas, found in Africa, Madagascar, the Middle East, southern Asia and the Australian region, plus eight families of lizards found in the Western Hemisphere, Madagascar, and Fiji. Some of these are the Basilisks, Horned and Fence Lizards, Collared Lizards, and true Iguanas.

The last lineage contains two major subgroups (some include the Worm Lizards in this). The first comprises the Gila Monster and Beaded Lizards, (the only venomous lizards), the Alligator Lizards, the Monitors, and the Xenosaurs. The rare and enigmatic Bornean Earless Lizard (*Lanthanotus borneensis*), well-illustrated for the first time in this book, is part of this assemblage. Monitors are found in southern Asia and the Old World tropics; the Xenosaurs (with one exception in China), Gila Monster and Beaded Lizards are found in North and Central America; and the Alligator Lizards and their allies are found in the Western Hemisphere, Europe, and southern Asia.

The last subgroup includes Girdle-tailed Lizards, Blind Lizards, Window-eyed Lizards, Lacertas, Skinks, Tegus and Racerunners, and the Night Lizards. Girdle-tailed Lizards live in sub-Saharan Africa and Madagascar. Blind Lizards occupy parts of China and Indonesia with a single species in Mexico. Window-eyed Lizards are found in Central and South America. Lacertas are found in Europe and Africa to Indo-Australia. Skinks are found throughout the world in temperate and tropical regions and are the most speciose group of lizards. Tegus and Racerunners are found in the Western Hemisphere, and Night Lizards are found from southern North America and Central America to Cuba.

Jackson's Chameleon *Chamaeleo jacksonii xantholophus*

Looking for all the world like a miniature dinosaur, or perhaps a rhinoceros, the male Jackson's Chameleon uses his equipment to joust with rivals. Females sport a single nubby spike on the snout. These harmless and comical lizards reach fourteen inches in length and are native to east Africa, with an introduced population in Hawaii. After fixing their turret-like eyes on an insect, the prey is captured with a sticky projectile tongue.

Flap-neck Chameleon
Chamaeleo dilepis dilepis

This moderately large (eight to fourteen inches) chameleon occurs in tropical Africa southward into Natal, Transvaal, and portions of Botswana, Cape Province, and Namibia. Principally an inhabitant of savanna woodland, it also occurs in coastal forest. They are often found in hedgerows and domestic gardens, where they hunt for beetles and grasshoppers. This species will inflate, gape, and bite readily when threatened. Perhaps because of this startling display, the Flap-neck is greatly feared by many tribes and is the object of much folklore. Aside from humans, predators include snakes, birds, and monkeys. Concealed by its coloration by day, the Flap-neck is easily located at night, its blue-white resting color standing out in the beam of a flashlight.

Minor's Chameleon *Furcifer minor*

Visible differences between males and females are not common among reptiles. However, in chameleons these differences are so marked that they verge on the humorous. Males, like many birds, are usually larger, more impressively bedecked with crests and horns, and sport gaudier colors and patterns. Males of the same species may be horned or hornless. Females carrying fertile eggs sometimes display a rainbow of colors to repel tardy suitors. After the female has deposited her clutch in the ground, her pattern will revert to a somber array of scattered bars and flecks. Minor's Chameleon is one of many unusual creatures to have evolved on Madagascar.

Poroto Chameleon
Chamaeleo fuelleborni

This eight-inch lizard is known only from the Ngosi Volcano region in the Poroto Mountains of Tanzania, Africa. An inhabitant of misty cane thickets and cloud forests at intermediate elevations, this chameleon is active by day. It forages for a variety of invertebrate prey.

Elephant Ear Chameleon *Calumma brevicornis*

Preferring humid, undisturbed forests in their native eastern Madagascar, these lizards possess flexible occipital lobes (fleshy flaps that can be extended laterally). When threatened, this species extends its lobes, giving the appearance of an elephant with its ears outstretched, inflates its body, and gapes. Large adult males can attain seven inches in length. Females are somewhat smaller. Females of this species have been reported to bury their eggs. The diet consists of insects.

Veiled Chameleon *Chamaeleo calyptratus*

The rocky steppes of Yemen and southwest Saudi Arabia are lands of extreme heat and little moisture. Yet this is home to one of the most spectacular of the chameleons. At nearly two feet in length, and bearing an imposing casque on its head, the Veiled Chameleon appears to wear a hat as it captures invertebrate prey with its sticky, protrusible tongue. It is believed that one function of its odd-looking head is conduction of condensed moisture to the mouth. At right, junior is "hitching a ride" with its parent.

BL

Panther Chameleon *Furcifer pardalis*

Above, Panther Chameleons, male (left) and female (right).

As forests in northern Madagascar are chopped down, this opportunist finds more of the open, sunny habitat it prefers. Thus, Panther Chameleons are an exception to the rule. They have actually benefitted from the rapacious inroads of humans. The pale pinkish brown females are dwarfed by their mates, which may exceed 20 inches in size. These lizards are as varied in hue as the land they occupy, with one race impressively adorned in blue, a color seldom seen in reptiles. The photos on this page and the next show some of the color variations.

PC

Chameleon eyes swivel independently and provide binocular vision, something unusual among reptiles. The bright eye colors and patterns of some species may aid in social interactions. They may also help the chameleon avoid the notice of its prey by breaking up the outline of the eye and thus making it difficult to detect. This is called disruptive coloration.

PC

Chameleons capture their prey through use of a remarkable, sticky projectile. Their tongues are protrusible, and the lizards extend them with deadly accuracy when hunting for food. Swivelling both turret-like eyes in a forward direction, the chameleon can achieve nearly binocular vision, a rare thing among reptiles, and much like someone aiming a rifle, direct its tongue at an unsuspecting insect. Upon impact, the hapless prey is drawn into the lizard's mouth by the recoiling tongue. The photos show the enormous length of the tongue and also how the sticky tip of the tongue is wrapped around the prey as it is drawn back to the mouth.

White-lined Chameleon

Furcifer antimena

This 12-inch chameleon is found only in southwestern Madagascar. It is distinguished by having a white line on its underside and a distinctive nasal appendage. An insect-eater, this species has been found to be active at night. Chameleons possess prehensile tails. They are flexible and aid in gripping surfaces as they clamber about in trees and bushes.

40

PC

Armored Chameleon *Brookesia perarmata*

This little gargoyle has been found in vegetation between rocks in its native western Madagascar. It is the most strongly spined and, at four inches, the largest member of its genus. Practically nothing is known of its natural history.

Pigmy Leaf Chameleon *Brookesia minima*

With a maximum size of less than two inches, this diminutive creature, along with some of the sphaerodactyline geckos of the neotropics, ranks among the world's smallest reptiles. Blending remarkably with leaves and twigs on the ground, these tiny Madagascan lizards also feign death to avoid predators.

BL

Parson's Chameleon

Calumma parsonii

Measuring nearly 24 inches, Parson's Chameleon is the most robust of its tribe. A denizen of the cool rainforest canopy in Madagascar, this species spends its days hunting for spiders, large insects, and lizards, all of which are captured with its long, sticky tongue. Unlike other members of the genus, the skin of the Parson's Chameleon resembles fine, crushed leather. In the photo above, the yellow Parson's Chameleon is the male. The female is green. The photos below and at right both show spectacular males.

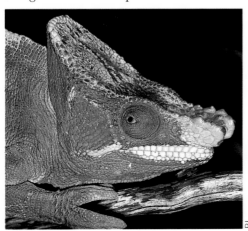

Madagascan Flap-necked
Chameleon *Calumma malthe*

Found throughout the length of eastern Madagascar, this species shares its unusual head shape with a variety of chameleons found on the African mainland. The neck flap can be erected and may form a part of this 12-inch lizard's defensive display. Like so many of the Madagascan chameleons, this species is very poorly known, and it may actually prove to be a composite, with other distinctive species as yet undetected under the same name. The photo above shows a male with his impressive nasal decorations.

Johnston's Chameleon
Chamaeleo johnstoni johnstoni

Like its close relative, the Jackson's Chameleon, males of this eleven-inch species engage in ritual combat, using the horns on their heads. Females, however, lack this ornamentation. Johnston's Chameleons are found in Africa, where they live in the rainforests of eastern Congo, and in neighboring Uganda, Rwanda, and Burundi.

GS

Jewel Chameleon *Furcifer campani* (above)

Described over 100 years ago by the French naturalist Guillaume Grandidier, this small chameleon is native to the uplands of Madagascar. It may be brown or pale green, with patterns of red spots and creamy stripes. Gravid females bear the brightest colors, perhaps to discourage amorous males. Like most chameleons, this species feeds on small insects.

Namaqua Chameleon *Chamaeleo namaquensis* (below)

Unlike most chameleons, this ten-inch lizard is primarily terrestrial, an adaptation to the harsh, nearly treeless environment where it lives. A native of Namaqualand and the Namib Desert of southern Africa, this reptile preys on a variety of invertebrates, small rodents, and other reptiles.

GS

PMF

Carpet Chameleon *Furcifer lateralis* (above)

Fear, excitement, and a host of other factors can cause this, perhaps the most variable of chameleons, to display a broad array of colors and patterns, sometimes changing in as little as ten seconds. Abundant in gardens, towns, and along roadsides in Madagascar's central highlands, this ten-inch lizard may produce over 100 eggs per year. Fortunately for the Carpet Chameleon, locals avoid it as an omen of bad luck.

Crevice Spiny Lizard *Sceloporus poinsetti poinsetti*

This 11-inch reptile is one of the largest of the spiny lizards, and it ranges through dry-to-desert regions from central Texas to New Mexico south to the Mexican state of Zacatecas. A denizen of rocky places, open or wooded, the Crevice Spiny Lizard has been found as high as 9000 feet above sea-level in the Guadalupe Mountains of west Texas. Alert and wary, this species feeds on insects and plant matter. Mating occurs in the Fall and females give birth to about ten young in late June. As with most members of the genus *Sceloporus*, males in breeding condition sport brilliant colors on their chins and bellies.

Common Chilean Swift

Liolaemus nigroviridis nigroviridis

Spiny lizards, often called "swifts," are creatures of dry regions. This swift is from northern Chile. The Andes of Chile in South America offer an abundance of habitats for lizards, especially those able to tolerate cold weather. Swifts have adapted to this and can be found from 7,500 feet above sea-level and higher in the mountains. These eight-inch lizards can be seen by day as they scamper about on rocks in zones of low, sparse vegetation. Their diet consists of insects, and the young are born alive. During cold seasons, these reptiles seek refuge under rocks and live on fatty reserves in their tails.

Emerald Swift

Sceloporus malachiticus

Part of a complex and poorly understood group of reptiles known collectively as spiny lizards, these iridescent, five-inch swifts live at intermediate to high elevations in the mountains of Central America. Often seen basking on posts like their US counterparts, the Fence Lizards, Emerald Swifts scurry like squirrels to the opposite side of their perches to hide from danger. Colorful males court the drab females and defend their territories through a series of postures.

Eastern Collared Lizard *Crotaphytus collaris*

Also known as "Mountain Boomers," collared lizards are colorful, 14-inch predators capable of running on their hind legs like tiny dinosaurs. Their large heads and heavy jaws allow them to subdue and consume smaller lizards, a favorite prey item. This reptile is a familiar sight on rocky outcrops throughout central and western North America.

Blue Spiny Lizard

Sceloporus serrifer cyanogenys

This is the largest member of the "fence lizard" group in the US and adjacent northeast Mexico. This swift predator hunts for insects while keeping a watchful eye out for racers, coachwhips, and other snakes that might eat it. Like many other species of spiny lizard, males take on brilliant blue and turquoise hues during the breeding season.

Frilled Lizard *Chlamydosaurus kingii*

Found in Australia and Irian Jaya, this is the reptile emblem of Australia, depicted on a coin and popularized in children's books. The frill can be quite large on the three-foot adults. The gaping lizard extends it as part of an intimidating bluff. If this fails, the animal beats a hasty retreat into a tree, where it clings motionless to the trunk and is hard to detect. Frilled lizards subsist on a diet of insects.

A view of this lizard with its frills relaxed.

Thorny Devil *Moloch horridus*

Certainly, this is the world's most bizarre lizard. Thorny Devils, despite their name and intimidating appearance, are gentle creatures that feed on ants. A Throny Devil can ingest up to 5,000 black ants at meal, lapping them up with its sticky tongue. Adapted for life in the hostile desert of inland Australia, this eight-inch reptile can alter its color and pattern to match its surroundings. Thorny Devils drink by collecting condensed water on their skin and funneling it to the corners of the mouth. Horned Lizards of the US (page 55) are remarkably similar to Thorny Devils.

Eastern Glass Lizard *Ophisaurus ventralis*

This is a lizard without legs, so it's no wonder that it is frequently mistaken for a snake. The careful observer will note that, unlike a snake, it possesses moveable eyelids and external ear openings. Reaching over three feet in length, this inoffensive occupant of the southeastern US feeds on a variety of insects, small vertebrates, and bird eggs.

When threatened, the Glass Lizard thrashes wildly and attempts to flee. However, if grasped, it changes tactics, often shedding its fragile tail, leaving a wriggling piece to distract its persecutor while it makes its escape. Like many other lizard species, the Eastern Glass Lizard can regenerate its tail, although never to its original size.

Giant Amphisbaena

Amphisbaena alba

Largest of the Amphisbaenians, or Worm-lizards, this powerful, two-foot reptile looks like a huge earthworm. Nearly blind, amphisbaenians spend most of their lives burrowing in loose soil and leaf litter, where they hunt for eggs, small vertebrates, and insects which make up their diet. Giant Amphisbaenas are found across much of northern South America, in both the Orinoco and Amazon Basins. The blunt tail looks much like the head, and when threatened, this reptile will raise both, perhaps to confuse a predator. Locals believe this creature possesses two heads.

Longnose Leopard Lizard

Gambelia wislizenii

Formerly common in its native western US, this inhabitant of arid regions has declined in recent years, probably because of habitat loss. Aptly named both for its spots and its predatory nature, the Leopard Lizard feeds primarily on other lizards.

Amazon Wood Lizard

Enyalioides laticeps

Wood Lizards are creatures of deep forest, living in the Upper Amazon Basin of South America. They spend much of the day sitting motionless in the brush, waiting for unsuspecting beetles or spiders to pass within reach.

Northern Caiman Lizard

Dracaena guianensis

One of the few aquatic lizards in the Amazon Basin, this imposing four-foot reptile is adorned with rugged scales that make it resemble its crocodilian namesake. Whether this benefit extends beyond similarity to providing actual protection is unknown. Adept swimmers, Caiman Lizards use their powerful jaws and specialized, rounded teeth to crush the shells of aquatic snails which form a major part of their diet. Interestingly, termite nests are used as sites for the deposit of eggs of this species. Caiman Lizards are harvested for their meat and hides.

PC

Rainbow Whiptail

Cnemidophorus lemniscatus lemniscatus

The coastal dunes, savannas and dry thornscrub of Central America and northern South America are populated with this eight-inch lizard. As males in breeding condition dart about during the day, their brilliant colors make them look like jewels. When actively hunting its insect prey, this reptile often pauses and waves a hand rhythmically before proceeding. No one knows the reason for this behavior.

Northern Monkey Lizard

Polychrus gutturosus

Sporting a tail longer than its body, this arboreal lizard moves, monkey-like, through the canopy of rainforests from Honduras south into western Ecuador. Although it can exceed 20 inches in length, this reptile is of delicate build. A patient stalker, it captures insects and small lizards as prey.

WL

Ornate Dabb-lizard

Uromastyx ocellatus ornatus

Barely one foot in length, this vegetarian likes it hot, turning on its brightest colors in the blaze of the morning sun. It is an inhabitant of rocky slopes and small mountain valleys with rich annual vegetation. A social reptile, the Ornate Dabb-lizard lives in colonies, foraging actively for insects and plant matter when the sun is shining, and passing cool evenings in burrows. When threatened, Dabb-lizards rush into their burrows and inflate their bodies so that they are difficult to remove. When cornered, the club-like tail is wielded with formidable accuracy. This robust lizard ranges through portions of Saudi Arabia, Egypt, Israel, and perhaps Syria. Adult males, like many desert lizards, are more brightly colored than the smaller females. These reptiles and their close relatives, the Bell's Dabb-lizards (*Uromastyx acanthinurus werneri*) have long been exploited as a food source, for medicine, and for leather. Strangely, in Morocco, live Dabb-lizards are used as shark-bait.

Northern Desert Horned Lizard
Phrynosoma platyrhinos platyrhinos

    Horned Lizards are adapted to rather harsh environments, favoring desert and scrub lands in dry regions. The Desert Horned Lizard can be found in the US in Utah, Nevada, eastern California, Idaho and southeastern Oregon. Ants are an important part of its diet. The Thorny Devil of Australia's desert, although not closely related, is similar in lifestyle and appearance.

Montane Horned Lizard
Acanthosaura armata

    This occupant of deep forests ranges through Southeast Asia from Thailand and Cambodia south through Sumatra and adjacent portions of Indonesia. Like chameleons and anoles, it can change its color, and adults may be brown, blackish, or green, sometimes spotted. An insect-eater, this lizard is said to prefer worms, which it exhumes by scaping with its forelimbs. Maximum length is about twelve inches.

Indochinese Bloodsucker *Calotes mystaceus*

Like most members of its genus, this 16-inch lizard is capable of remarkable color changes, especially the males in breeding condition. It makes its home in tropical and lower montane forest. It is known to occur in Yunnan, China, the Andaman and Nicobar Islands of India, and from Myanmar (Burma) to Thailand, Cambodia, Vietnam, and parts of Malaysia.

Blue-tailed Tree Lizard *Holaspis guentheri laevis*

This five-inch lizard with the unusual, flattened tail is native to humid forests across equatorial Africa. An adept climber, it hunts for ants and spiders on the trunks of trees. It also is at home in the canopy, where it escapes predators by climbing rapidly, jumping, and even gliding between trees. Females deposit two eggs per clutch.

Armadillo Girdled Lizard
Cordylus cataphractus

Well-protected by its formidable scaly covering, the Armadillo Lizard evades predators by rolling into a ball and grasping its tail in its mouth. Few animals would remain interested in such a spiny and unappetizing object. This eight-inch repitle lives in dry, open regions near the southwestern tip of Africa, often in family groups that occupy rocky outcrops. Heavily persecuted for the pet trade, this insect-eater gives birth to only one or two babies per year.

Western Chuckwalla *Sauromalus obesus obesus*

One of North America's largest lizards is frequently seen in the deserts of the western US, where it tends to bask on sun-baked, rocky outcrops. A vegetarian, the Chuckwalla feeds on a variety of fruits, flowers, and leaves. When alarmed, this 16-inch lizard retreats into rocky crevices and inflates its body so that it becomes nearly impossible to remove. The Western Chuckwalla is native to harsh, dry regions in the American Southwest and adjacent Mexico.

PC

Web-footed Gecko *Palmatogecko rangei*

This five-inch "ghost of the dunes" is so superbly adapted to life in its native Namib desert of southern Africa that it can slip through the sand leaving barely a trail. Like snowshoes, its webbed feet allow this slender lizard to glide across the sand without sinking. Other adaptations to its harsh desert home include tubular nostrils and pupils that can close to a pinhole in bright light. Emerging at night from their burrows, Web-footed Geckos hunt for spiders and insects, obtaining all of their moisture from prey items and condensing fog.

The photo at right shows a Web-footed Gecko using its tongue to clean its eye. This common behavior can be seen in several other photos in this section.

PMF

PMF

Introduction to Geckos

Geckos, with their soft skin, bizarre eyes, specialized feet, and often brilliant colors, are among the most distinctive of the lizards.

Special toe pads containing microscopic hooks allow some geckos to climb over almost any surface.

Some of the smallest reptiles in the world are geckos (*Lepidoblepharis* and *Sphaerodactylus* are less than one inch long), while larger species may be as much as sixteen inches in length. Habitats include forest, desert, and even houses. Some species are capable of vocalization. Most geckos are egg layers, and the majority are insect-eaters.

Mossy Leaftail Gecko

Uroplatus sikorae sameiti

Leaftail geckos are found only on Madagascar, where they hunt by night for insect prey. Highly specialized, with large, triangular heads and bulbous eyes, these twelve-inch creatures have such a startling appearance that many locals fear them. The Mossy Leaftail Gecko is found in the eastern forests where it bears a striking resemblance to a moss-and-lichen encrusted tree trunk.

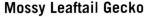

59

Giant Leaftail Gecko *Uroplatus fimbriatus* (above)

Frilled Leaftail Gecko *Uroplatus henkeli* (above, and below)

Frilled Leaftail Gecko

Uroplatus henkeli

This Madagascan native is a master at hiding, with its dermal flaps and fringes making it difficult to distinguish from the bark upon which it perches. At night this ten-inch predator waits motionless to ambush unwary insects. Marble-sized eggs are laid in pairs, several times per year, in the damp leaf litter of its virgin forest habitat. Hatchlings resemble adults and can mature in one year.

Satanic Leaftail Gecko *Uroplatus phantasticus*

It is easy to imagine how this lizard from Madagascar, with its wild-looking red eyes, horns, and strange, spear-tipped tail, might be called Satanic, but there is nothing evil about it. It is completely harmless. These lizards live in moist forests where they hop, rather than run, along the ground. Only three or four inches in length, these insect-eaters hide among low vegetation.

Mossy Leaftail Gecko *Uroplatus sikorae sameiti* (see description, page 59)

Common Flying Gecko *Ptychozoon kuhli*

"Gliding Gecko" might be a more appropriate name for this arboreal, six-inch lizard from Southeast Asia. It has superb camouflage, reminiscent of the Leaftail Geckos of Madagascar.

However, when its camouflage fails, this reptile can leap and glide to safety using its lateral fringes and wide toes like a parachute. The head-down position shown here is this gecko's normal resting posture when clinging to the trunk of a tree.

Day Geckos *Phelsuma sp.*

There are about three dozen species within this remarkable group of insect- and nectar-eating lizards. They are endemic (native) to the Indian Ocean region. Ranging from a few inches to nearly a foot in length, these inquisitive reptiles are gaily colored in brilliant greens, blues, yellows, reds, oranges, and tans. Madagascar boasts the greatest diversity, with 20 resident species, but the range extends from Tanzania east to the Andaman Islands, near Thailand. Many of the day geckos thrive in altered habitats and can be found in cultivated areas, or around human habitation.

Four-eyed Day Gecko *Phelsuma quadriocellata lepida*

At under five inches, this is a small day gecko species. It ranges throughout eastern Madagascar in suitable habitat. Females, during the breeding season, may produce as many as six sets of two eggs each.

Standing's Day Gecko *Phelsuma standingi* (below)

One of the largest of the Day Geckos, this spectacular lizard is restricted to forest bordering the Onilahy river and adjacent regions in arid southwest Madagascar. Females deposit two soft eggs which are adhered in crevices for the two-month incubation period. Hatchlings are brightly banded, becoming speckled with maturity. The green heads and aquamarine tails of the adults intensify when basking. Under protection by local law, the population status of these reptiles is uncertain and in need of scientific evaluation.

Giant Day Gecko

Phelsuma madagascariensis grandis

At 12 inches, this is the largest and certainly one of the most spectacular of the day geckos. Found on and around houses and cultivated areas in humid north Madagascar, this prolific lizard can produce up to ten clutches of one to two eggs per season. Like many geckos, its skin tears easily, a fact which enables it to escape predators.

Most geckos have large eyes, and in some species the lids are fused to form a transparent, protective shield. Since these geckos cannot blink, they use their long tongues to lick debris from their eyes (and face).

Gold-dust Day Gecko

Phelsuma laticauda laticauda

This five-inch reptile abounds in its native northern Madagascar. Preferring banana gardens but also occupying open spots within primary (uncut) rainforest, this is a fast-growing species, and it can reach maturity in less than one year. The common name derives from the fine golden speckles present on the neck.

64

Blue-tail Day Gecko *Phelsuma cepediana*

This delicate lizard, with its brilliant blue back and tail, lives in the Mascarene Islands. Introduced and apparently spreading in Madagascar, it has been found on both coasts. It is fortunate that these geckos can adapt to areas altered by humans, as most of their native habitat, especially on the island of Mauritius, has been severely decimated. As much as six inches in length, this species prefers humid regions. The blue pigment adorning mature males is an uncommon color in reptiles.

Neon Day Gecko *Phelsuma klemmeri* (below)

Nearly all the Day Geckos are green, due to the combination of yellow and blue pigments. Not so with this dainty three and one-half inch beauty. When fully warmed by the sun, its colors appear most intense. Regarded as endangered, this recently discovered species lives in a restricted habitat, the forest along the northwest coast of Madagascar. An insect- and nectar-feeder, the Neon Day Gecko is currently being bred in captive programs.

Central American Banded Gecko
Coleonyx mitratus

An inhabitant of dry thornscrub and deciduous forests from southern Guatemala to Panama, the Central American Banded Gecko is nocturnal and terrestrial. This delicate, 4-inch lizard hides by day in burrows or crevices, emerging at dusk to prowl and hunt for insects. When threatened, it elevates its body, arches its tail, opens its mouth slightly, and emits squeaking sounds. Often when running, this gecko resembles a scorpion because of its arched tail.

African Fat-tailed Gecko
Hemitheconyx caudicinctus

During lean times, this eight-inch lizard survives by consuming the fat reserves it stores in its tail. Slow moving and terrestrial, these reptiles live in humid regions of western Africa where they feed on small insects. Females are prolific egg layers and may produce up to 20 eggs per year.

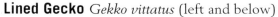

Lined Gecko *Gekko vittatus* (left and below)

This rainforest species, at ten inches in length, is one of the larger geckos. It is native to the Indo-Australian Archipelago, from Java through Oceania. Insects and small vertebrates make up the diet of this nocturnal reptile.

Leopard Gecko

Eublepharis macularius

These geckos, which have been known to breed at the ripe old age of fifteen years, lay eggs in pairs, five to ten times per season. When stalking their insect prey, Leopard Geckos often wriggle their tail-tip, much as a cat does. This eight-inch lizard lives in dry environments from Afghanistan and Pakistan east to India. It has been found at nearly 7000 feet above sea-level. The photo at right is a juvenile while the photo at top is an adult.

Tokay Gecko *Gekko gecko*

The word "gecko" derives from one of the distinctive calls of this twelve-inch, voracious insect-eater. The name "Tokay" comes from one of its several other calls. The Tokay Gecko is native to Southeast Asia. Like most geckos, it often travels as a stowaway. Since it is also a popular reptile because it controls insects, the Tokay has had little problem in becoming established in numerous tropical locales around the world. Hiding by day, often in roofs of human habitations, Tokays use communal nesting sites in which their paired eggs are glued to vertical surfaces.

Eastern Three-lined
Knob-tail *Nephrurus levis levis*

This feisty six-inch gecko is native to Australia's arid interior, where it shelters by day in a tunnel it constructs on the side of another animal's burrow. It even make a "door" out of sand in order to close its tunnel. Its preferred habitat is tropical sand plains, dunes and shrub land. When threatened, the Knob-tail makes mock attacks.

Striped Frog-eyed Gecko
Teratoscincus scincus keyzerlingii

It is surprising that a creature as delicate as a gecko, with skin like velvet, and soft liquid eyes, can eke out an existence in the harsh, dry heat of the desert. The five-inch Striped Frog-Eyed Gecko relies on the protective coolness of its 30-inch burrow and the sand-shedding ability of its "eyelashes," toe-fringes, and overlapping body scales. The milder temperatures at night suit this nocturnal insect-eater. It is found in Southwest and Central Asia.

Eastern Bluetongue Skink
Tiliqua scincoides scincoides

Reaching 18 inches in length, this robust Australian lizard is one of the world's largest skinks. This species is shiny and slow-moving. When threatened it is prone to gape suddenly and display its blue-colored tongue. The striking appearance of the tongue presumably aids in deterring predators. These hardy creatures thrive on a diet of insects, small vertebrates, and vegetable matter, and they are a familiar sight to most Australians.

Eastern Shingle-back *Trachydosaurus rugosus asper*

Arguably Australia's most familiar lizard, this unique, 15-inch reptile is often seen crossing roads. Because of its distinctive demeanor, scalation and peculiar shape, Australians have a multitude of names for the Shingle-back. Among others it is known as "Sleepy Lizard", "Bob-tail", and "Double-ender." This lizard ranges through South Australia, Victoria, New South Wales, and Queensland. Shingle-backs occupy a wide variety of habitat, both open areas and woodland. They feed on insects, fruits, carrion, mollusks, flowers, and berries.

Fire Skink *Lygosoma fernandi*

A burrow dweller, this robust, attractive skink makes its home in west African forests. Little is known of its behavior and ecology. Like many lizards, Fire Skinks can shed their bright blue and black tails if grasped by a predator, and the wriggling appendage can be an effective distraction to their enemies. If that fails, these powerful foot-long skinks can bite with surprising strength. Perhaps due to their brilliant coloration, this species is erroneously believed by locals to be poisonous.

Golden Skink
Eumeces schneideri aldrovandii

The Golden Skink can exceed 18 inches in length. Adapted to a variety of environments, this lizard ranges across north Africa to the Sinai Peninsula. The Golden Skink is active during the day, but retreats into its burrow during the hottest hours. The pugnacious males battle each other vigorously on sight. Its diet includes various invertebrates and small lizards.

71

Dumeril's Monitor *Varanus dumerilii dumerilii*

This reptile is member of the family that includes the world's largest lizards. It ranges through mangrove swamps and evergreen forests in tropical situations from Thailand and West Malaysia through Sarawak and Indonesia. Like most monitors, Dumeril's is fond of water, but it is an adept climber as well, although generally it occupies the forest floor or low bushes. Its diet includes insects, frogs, crabs and fish, but at four feet in length, the adults are capable of capturing sizeable prey items. These they dispatch with crushing jaw-pressure. Females produce about 12 eggs per year, and the juveniles emerge with brilliant orange heads and bright yellow bands on their bodies.

Introduction to Monitors

Monitors occupy a diversity of habitats, ranging from desert to lush rainforest. Some are semi-aquatic. All are carnivorous, and all are egg-layers. Monitors are restricted to the Old World, where most are found along the tropical belt.

Blue-tailed Monitor

Varanus doreanus doreanus

This beautiful, four-foot species was rediscovered during the 1990's after a long period of neglect. It is referred to by some as Kalabeck's Monitor. It requires rainforest habitat where it forages for eggs, carrion and small vertebrates. It is found from Irian Jaya, Indonesia, to Papua, New Guinea.

Crocodile Monitor
Varanus salvadorii

This denizen of coastal mangroves and dry forest along the southern coast of Papua and Irian Jaya on the island of New Guinea is one of the world's most enigmatic reptiles. It was seldom seen for many years and even today is poorly known. Often rumored to be the world's longest lizard, it is true that a record of over 15 feet does exist. However, the specimen was not deposited in a museum so it cannot be verified. This species normally reaches lengths of at least eight feet. It is slender and uses its excessively long tail when climbing. Its diet includes birds and their eggs as well as other vertebrates.

ROBIN COLE/ECO-STOCK

BK

Nile Monitor *Varanus niloticus ssp.*

Largest and best-known of Africa's monitor lizards, this six-foot predator ranges throughout most of the continent. Favoring moist situations, these reptiles are known for their habit of stealing eggs from crocodile nests along riverbanks. Nile Monitors are powerful, consuming practically anything they can overcome. With their strong claws, they excavate termite mounds to use as nests. When threatened, Nile Monitors defend themselves capably with their teeth, claws, and whip-like tail. This species has been exploited as a source of meat, hides, and for the pet trade for many years.

JOSE' AZEL/AURORA

Komodo Monitor *Varanus komodoensis*

The most massive living lizard, large males can exceed ten feet and 200 pounds. Restricted to a few islands in the middle of the Lesser Sunda group, Republic of Indonesia, these reptiles are the dominant predators within their range, feeding on a wide variety of vertebrates, including deer and boar. They are also scavengers, and are adept at locating carrion. Even others of their own kind are not safe, and smaller specimens will often shelter in trees for protection from the larger adults. There are documented instances of attacks by this species on man, although such activity must be regarded as unusual. Komodo Monitors are active by day, but spend the night in burrows they excavate into hillsides.

SO

74

Common Monkey Lizard *Polychrus marmoratus*

With its turret-like eyes, partially prehensile tail, and slow demeanor, the Monkey Lizard is reminiscent of the Old World chameleons. However, this 15-inch tree dweller comes from South America, where it is found throughout the Orinoco and Amazon Basins as well as in Brazil's Atlantic forest. These lizards spend most of their lives in trees, either in the tropical forest canopy or in shrubs and forest-edge situations. A variety of insects and even small lizards constitutes their diet.

PC

Southern Green Anole (blue phase)
Anolis carolinensis seminolus

These eight-inch lizards are known to many in the US as "chameleons," although the resemblance is purely superficial. However, they can change color from green (or blue, in the case of the blue phase) to brown. A common daytime sight in gardens of the US southeast, these insect-eaters engage in territorial and mating rituals, with males displaying a pink or gray dewlap (see photo at right for a view of another anole's dewlap). Some individuals lack yellow pigment in the skin, resulting in their blue color. This anomaly has been documented in other green animals such as Bullfrogs and Green Tree Pythons.

Mayan Coastal Anole *Anolis sagrei ssp.*

This eight-inch lizard is native to Cuba, the Bahama Islands, Jamaica, Isla de la Juventud, Swan Island, the Cayman Islands, the Atlantic coast of Mexico south to Limón, Costa Rica, and associated cays and small islands elsewhere in the Caribbean. It was first detected in the Florida Keys many years ago. Today, a thriving, expanding population of these lizards has colonized the Keys and moved northward into central Florida. Brown Anoles do not climb as high nor as often as their relatives the Southern Green Anoles. They run rapidly with an erratic gait. Females deposit one egg, about every two weeks, in leaf litter or other protected areas. This habit may have resulted in this lizard being widely distributed in Florida. Eggs deposited in landscaping pots were probably shipped to many parts of the state. Abounding in open seaside habitats, these lizards beat a hasty retreat into hedges and fence rows when threatened. Insects make up their diet.

GS

Banded Tree Anole

Anolis transversalis

Its bright blue eyes and bold, banded pattern make this one of the Amazon's most beautiful anoles. Found only in trees and saplings in rainforest, the Banded Tree Anole is unusual in that the females are as spectacularly colored as the males, bearing even bolder patterns and a large, well-marked dewlap. Reaching 12 inches in length, this lizard feeds on small insects and is active by day.

Knight Anole *Anolis equestris*

Measuring up to 18 inches in length, Knight Anoles, also known as Giant Cuban Anoles, are the largest and most impressive members of their tribe. Native to the island of Cuba, this species was introduced into Coral Gables, Florida, many decades ago. Now, in the giant banyan trees lining the streets and yards in the elegant old neighborhoods of this community, it is possible to see this spectacular and beautiful lizard perched and surveying its domain. Active by day, Knight Anoles are fierce and aggressive predators, capturing insects and lizards and deterring their enemies with their formidable dentition.

PC

Plumed Basilisk *Basiliscus plumifrons*

Looking like a modern version of the dinosaur *Dimetrodon*, an adult male Plumed Basilisk, resplendent in green and sporting an impressive array of crests, makes an unforgettable image. Inhabitants of low bushes lining waterways in lowland regions of Nicaragua, Costa Rica, and Panama, these two-foot lizards hunt by day for invertebrates, amphibians, and small mammals. They are equipped with long toes and sharp claws.

Spiny Helmeted Basilisk *Corytophanes hernandesi*

A creature of the shadows, this dramatic lizard makes its home in the moist rainforests of southeastern Mexico, Belize, and Guatemala. Reaching about ten inches in length, the Spiny Helmeted Basilisk spends the day in search of small insects that comprise its diet. When detected, these reptiles often remain motionless, their somber colors and unusual outline blending perfectly with their surroundings.

BK

Stephen Dalton/NHPA

Brown Basilisk *Basiliscus vittatus*

Basilisks are capable of astonishing bursts of speed, and can even run across spans of open water when fleeing danger. This has earned them the nickname, "Jesus Christ Lizard." The Brown Basilisk is a familiar sight to residents of Central America from southeastern Mexico south to Colombia and possibly Ecuador. Although this species can grow up to two feet in length, it averages considerably less. Like other Basilisks, it favors rivers and streams, often living in open areas. Its food is made up of insects and small vertebrates.

Elegant Helmeted Basilisk

Corytophanes cristatus

Shape, in addition to color, can aid in concealment. This 12-inch, insect-eating, helmeted lizard remains motionless when detected in its native rainforests of Central and western South America. With its color and odd silhouette, it is amazingly difficult to see this harmless reptile as it perches among the shrubbery.

PC

Green Iguana *Iguana iguana*

A classically familiar reptile to most people, the Green Iguana has been of much use to humans. Within their Latin American habitat, these large vegetarians are sought after for their meat, eggs, and hides. For many years their numbers as pets have been increasing (unfortunately, often with little knowledge of how to care for them). They have served as film subjects in dinosaur and monster movies. There are "iguana parks" catering to the tourist trade in several countries. It would appear that iguanas are well on their way to becoming domesticated.

Commercial breeding ventures have recently been successful. Adult females, which may measure up to six feet in length, lay two to six dozen eggs annually, often nesting on sandy beaches used by crocodiles and caimans. Babies are eight to twelve inches long at birth and brilliant green in color. Adult males often take on a beautiful orange hue during their breeding season.

KS

PC

Fijian Banded Iguana *Brachylophus fasciatus*

A truly exotic creature, the Fijian Banded Iguana lives only in the Fiji Islands of the southwest Pacific Ocean. This docile, 30-inch vegetarian engages in ritual combat and breathtaking color displays involved with mating and territoriality. Due to its limited range, this gorgeous reptile enjoys protected status. Few specimens exist in captivity. It may be interbreeding in the wild with the only closely related species, the Fijian Crested Iguana.

Black Spinytail Iguana
(juvenile)
Ctenosaura similis

This robust lizard is common in coastal regions from southeastern Mexico to Panama. Feeding on a wide variety of vegetable matter and occasionally meat, the Black Spinytail Iguana has become a familiar sight to vacationers and campers in Costa Rica, where it frequents picnic areas in hopes of a handout. Large adult males can reach three feet in length, and they develop massive heads that appear too large for their bodies. In breeding condition, males may be orange to sky-blue, unlike the green juveniles.

PC

Marine Iguana
Amblyrhynchus cristatus ssp.

The salty marine environment is home to very few reptiles. Of those, the Marine Iguana, with its prehistoric appearance and exotic home in Ecuador's Galapagos Islands, has become a familiar sight to many. This vegetarian uses specialized teeth to graze algae from intertidal rock surfaces. Each island boasts a distinct race of Marine Iguana, and they range from two to five feet in length. Territorial by day, these interesting reptiles form large sleeping piles by night, presumably to conserve heat. Like so many of the creatures on the Galapagos, this species is docile and can be approached closely by man.

Galapagos Land Iguana *Conolophus subcristatus*

This robust lizard is found only on the islands of Santiago, Santa Cruz, Isabela, Fernandina, Plazas, and North Seymour, in the Galapagos Archipelago of Ecuador. Males, which greatly exceed females in size, can weigh over 25 lbs on some islands, while on others they may only reach half that size. These lizards are primarily vegetarians, although animal matter is consumed if easily accessible. During breeding season, males engage in fierce battles with one another, usually over territorial disputes. Aside from man, the only enemies this lizard must face are a single species of snake and a single hawk species, and these are only capable of preying on hatchlings.

Mwanza Rock Agama *Agama mwanzae*

This 16-inch lizard was long considered to be a race of the wide-ranging Common Agama. However, it has recently been accorded full species ranking. It is found only in east Africa where it occurs in open, rocky situations in northwest Tanzania.

Blue-throated Tree Lizard *Laudakia atricollis*

This lizard ranges from Ethiopia across sub-Saharan Africa in the equatorial belt. It is somewhat arboreal and seen around forest edges where it hunts insects by day.

Egyptian Hardun *Laudakia stellio vulgaris*

This lizard, one of six races, is found in northern Egypt in rocky places where it shelters in crevices and feeds on insects.

Bearded Dragon

Pogona vitticeps

This impressive, 16-inch lizard lives in dry regions in central Australia, occupying a broad range of habitats. Semi-arboreal, Bearded Dragons are often seen as they perch on roadside fenceposts. When cornered, these reptiles put on a bluff display, expanding their throat, and gaping with their "beard" (actually, a fringe of scales) bristling. The photo at right illustrates this display. The photo at the top of the page shows the red color-phase of this lizard. These insect-eaters may produce up to several dozen eggs in the course of a year.

Introduction to Dragons

While there are no true "dragons" in the fire-breathing sense, many lizards are popularly given this common name. This does not necessarily mean that these creatures are related in appearance or behavior. This word has been used to describe creatures as diverse as the giant Komodo Monitor as well as the foot-long Bearded Lizard.

Javan Forest Dragon *Gonocephalus chamaeleontinus*

The genus *Gonocephalus* includes some of the most spectacular lizards in the world. The breeding coloration on mature males is striking. The Javan Forest Dragon is native to rainforests of West Malaysia, Sumatra, Java, and several smaller islands. It feeds on insects and is adept at climbing. Adults average about ten inches in length. When threatened, this species gapes and erects its dewlap. Females deposit their eggs in moist humus.

BK

Green Water Dragon *Physignathus concincinus*

    Although it bears casual resemblance to the Green Iguana of the western hemisphere, this two-foot reptile is actually a member of a different family. Water dragons are omnivores, including a broad range of items in their diet. They make their home in the dense foliage along water courses in Thailand, southwest China, and possibly Myanmar (Burma).

New Guinea Crocodile Skink *Tribolonotus gracilis*

    This seven-inch skink looks like something from a science fiction movie. Native to humid forest in Papua and Irian Jaya on the island of New Guinea, this sluggish, nocturnal lizard lives near streams in remote mountain valleys. It is an egg-layer, and both sexes possess unique glands beneath the ventral scales. Unfortunately, the purpose of these glands remains a mystery.

PC

Sungazer *Cordylus giganteus*

Largest of the Girdled Lizards at 16 inches, the spiky Sungazer makes quite an impression as it basks at the entrance to its burrow, or on a termite mound in its native South Africa. These reptiles live in colonies, usually in individual burrows, on grassy flat lands. Some colonies may number into the hundreds of individuals. Females give birth to one or two young which are brilliant black, orange, and yellow. They become a uniform tan at maturity. Once warmed by the sun, these armored lizards forage for insects and small vertebrates. When threatened, the Sungazer retreats into its burrow, lashing its spiny tail and embedding it into the roof of the tunnel. Sungazers are declining because of the large amount of land converted to sunflower farms.

Amazon Thornytail *Tropidurus (Uracentron) flaviceps*

Thornytails are among the most unusual lizards in the Amazon Basin. They are sociable, living in family groups in large trees where they shelter in holes and arboreal ant nests. These lizards average five to seven inches in length. They are extremely alert, and dart about catching tree ants, beetles, and an assortment of other invertebrates. This species is found in Brazil, Colombia, Ecuador, Peru, and possibly northern Bolivia.

Northern Tegu *Tupinambis teguixin*

There are five species of tegu. All are large, and all are found in South America. The Northern Tegu ranges over all of the continent as far south as Bolivia and Brazil. It is a ground-dweller, and occupies both forest and more open regions. Active on the ground during daylight, this lizard forages widely for food, which consists of leaves, fruits, invertebrates, eggs, and almost any vertebrate small enough to be subdued. It is known to excavate the eggs of sideneck turtles from sandy beaches. With large males reaching nearly 40 inches, this is a powerful and imposing reptile. When threatened, the Northern Tegu runs away rapidly, even crossing short stretches of water. If cornered, it defends itself with its strong jaws and sharp teeth.

Western Green Thornytail (adult male, left, hatchling above)
Tropidurus (Uracentron) azureum werneri

Thornytails, because of their treetop habitat, are seldom seen by humans. In addition, the Western Green Thornytail occupies a fairly remote sector of the Amazon Basin, in eastern Colombia, southern Venezuela, and adjacent Brazil. It is revered by some indigenous groups and feared by others as venomous (although it is harmless).

Long-tailed Lizard *Latastia longicaudata longicaudata*

This slender, foot-long lizard lives in exposed steppes and other zones of sparse vegetation and sandy soil. It ranges through north Africa in the Sinai region and into southwestern Arabia. The race depicted here is found in Egypt and the Sinai peninsula.

Reticulate Gila Monster *Heloderma suspectum suspectum*

Along with the Beaded Lizard of Mexico and Guatemala, the Gila Monster is the only venomous lizard. Boldly marked with pink or orange and black, at two feet in length, this species is one of the largest and most attractive lizards in the US. Long afforded government protection, this imposing reptile has become a classic symbol of the Mojave desert, where it lives in moist situations. Its potent venom, conducted via the lower jaw, appears to be primarily for defense, as the Gila Monster feeds on small mammals, birds, and eggs (for which it will climb trees). If molested, this species will flee, or gape and hiss, biting only as a last resort. Few bites on humans have been documented, and nearly all were the result of mishandling, but a bite can be a serious matter. These reptiles spend most of their time in burrows, being active primarily when high heat is not a factor. One to eight eggs are laid in July or August.

Bornean Earless Lizard *Lanthanotus borneensis*

One of the world's rarest and most enigmatic creatures, the foot-long Bornean Earless Lizard occupies near mythological status in the scientific community, largely because so few people have ever even seen a specimen. Found in Sarawak and a remote part of Kalimantan, Borneo, this bizarre reptile apparently lives in estuarine situations or flooded rice fields. It turns up in fishermen's nets. Nocturnal in habits and an egg layer, this sluggish lizard has puzzled systematists for years. Thought by some to be related to the monitors, and by others to the Gila Monster and Beaded Lizards, most place this reptile into a family by itself.

Amazon Whiptail *Ameiva ameiva*

"Lightning on four legs" aptly describes these swift, ground-dwelling lizards of tropical America. The many species range from a scant six inches to nearly two feet in length. Using their powerful legs, these reptiles capture unwary insects and small lizards with a burst of speed. When males are in breeding coloration they look like bright jewels as they dart about by day in search of food and mates.

Central American Whiptail *Ameiva festiva*

This ten-inch lizard is found in moist tropical forests from southeastern Mexico to Panama. The brilliantly-colored juveniles become somewhat darker with age. Insects make up its diet.

*T*he closest relatives to the lizards arose at least 135 million years ago. Their limblessness likely descended from burrowing adaptations. Some lizards may superficially resemble snakes because they also lack limbs and eyelids, and are covered in scales; but snakes possess many features that they do not share with lizards. The jaw of a snake is not fused, but is composed of two bones which can swing laterally to accommodate wide meals. Snakes use only one lung, lack external ear openings, have a protective eye covering, and most have enlarged scales on the belly to aid in locomotion. Although they are limbless, boas and pythons have vestigial hind-legs in the form of spurs, and blindsnakes also possess skeletal remnants of a pelvis.

There are at least 2600 species of snakes, and they are found on all continents except Antartica. Snakes are not found in Ireland, nor are many found within the Arctic Circle. They occupy a wide range of habitats including temperate and tropical forests, plains and savannas, mountains, oceans, deserts, oceanic islands, rivers, swamps, and marshes. Some species of snakes exist above 14,000 feet. There are arboreal (tree dwelling) snakes, blindsnakes that live underground, sea snakes, snakes that glide between trees, and snakes that live in swamps. Snakes range in size from six-inch blindsnakes to colossal constrictors like the Green Anaconda (*Eunectes murinus*) and the Reticulated Python (*Python reticulata*) that can reach 30 feet.

Snakes smell through their noses and especially via their forked tongues, which pass particles into a specialized organ for analysis. Some species have infrared sensors located in pits along their lip scales or at the front of their head. These aid in detecting prey and determining its size. Snakes as a group are carnivores, and many are generalists, feeding on reptiles, amphibians, birds, and mammals. Some snakes have a diet which changes as they age. Prey is captured by a strike and is either swallowed alive, constricted, or subdued with venom. Venomous snakes, although far out-numbered by harmless varieties, are found on all continents and in the sea. In many areas, the number of human deaths from snakebite is significant. Venomous species either possess flexible front fangs, permanently erect front fangs, or fangs in the rear of the mouth.

Snakes are preyed upon by all kinds of organisms, and they defend themselves with camouflage, cryptic coloration, biting, envenoming, hissing and puffing, feigning death, speedy retreat, gaping, rattling, and scale rubbing. A few kinds can lose their tails.

For snakes, fertilization is internal. Some species lay their eggs in humus, some brood their eggs, while others give birth to live young by one of three methods. Parental care is not common and the young are capable of fending for themselves from birth. In most species the sexes are only subtly distinguishable. Some species engage in combat rituals between males at mating time.

Snakes are ectotherms, generating most of their body temperature by accommodating to their surroundings. Some species can elevate their body heat by contracting muscles while brooding eggs.

Throughout history, many humans have felt a special revulsion toward snakes, a phenomenon that continues today. This is unfortunate and largely undeserved. Snakes have been associated with evil and a host of other negative human traits which actually play no part in a snake's existence. Snakes hold mythical and important positions in indigenous cosmologies throughout the world. They are probably the subject of more wild speculation than any other animal on earth. It is true that certain venomous species have caused a lot of human suffering. But the human onslaught against snakes continues as snakes are slaughtered for the hide trade, killed out of fear and ignorance, killed crossing roads, and eliminated through loss of habitat.

Snakes are usually classified into two large groups. The first, including Blindsnakes and Thread Snakes, is largely tropical, distributed world-wide, and contains slender to extremely slender snakes that are nearly sightless. Most lead a subterranean life and feed on ants and termites. The second group might be called Typical Snakes and consists of 15 families. Among those that are part of this group are the primitive Pipe Snakes, Boas, the New World Python, Pythons, Wood Snakes, Shield-tail and Sunbeam Snakes, and Wart Snakes. Also included are the colubrids, which contain most of the familiar and harmless varieties of snakes: racers, whipsnakes, gartersnakes, kingsnakes, ratsnakes, and watersnakes. But this family also contains dangerously venomous species: Africa's Boomslang (*Dispholidus typus*) and Twig Snake (*Thelotornis kirtlandi*). Families containing the venomous Burrowing Vipers, the Kraits, Cobras, Coralsnakes and Seasnakes, and the Vipers and Pitvipers (including Rattlesnakes) are the last part of this lineage.

Among the non-venomous snakes, most pythons are found in the Old World tropics, while boas occupy the Western Hemisphere, Africa, Madagascar, and parts of Asia. Ratsnakes, Racers, and Whipsnakes are found from North and Central America to China. Garter, Ribbon, and Kingsnakes inhabit the Western Hemisphere. Pitvipers are found in the Western Hemisphere, the Pacific, and parts of Asia, with one variety barely appearing in western Europe. Coralsnakes are unique to the Western Hemisphere, while Kraits and Cobras are found only in the Old World. Australia's venomous snake fauna is related to the cobras. Seasnakes are primarily found in the southwest Pacific, but one, the Pelagic or Yellow-bellied Seasnake (*Pelamis platurus*) is the widest ranging snake in the world, and the only seasnake to reach the Western Hemisphere.

Amazon Tree Boa
Corallus hortulanus

PC

Rhinoceros Adder *Bitis nasicornis*

Although it may seem strange, the gaudy colors and complex pattern of this denizen of equatorial African forests actually help with its camouflage. They effectively disrupt the outline so that the small mammals on which it feeds will pass within striking range. A "lie-and-wait" predator, the three-foot Rhinoceros Adder ambushes its prey either on the forest floor or in low bushes, where it climbs to considerable heights in spite of its heavy build. When its prey has been deeply and fatally injected, the long fangs assist in swallowing by "walking" the food into the snake's throat. The venom aids in digestion.

West African Gaboon Adder
Bitis gabonica rhinoceros

Corpulent, gaudy, and nearly undetectable as it lies motionless in the leaf litter of the forest floor, this African snake is one of the world's heaviest venomous snakes. Its enormous fangs can measure over two inches in length in specimens of six feet or more, and the venom, borne in large quantity, is particularly virulent. Fortunately, due to its restriction to rainforests and its placid nature, bites to humans are rare. Ambushing their prey as they lie among the leaves, Gaboon Adders feed primarily upon mammals. The young are born alive, with up to 60 snakes in a litter.

PC

KS

Sahara Horned Viper *Cerastes cerastes*

Superbly adapted for life in the inhospitable climate of the desert, this 30-inch, sand-colored snake can be found from from Yemen and the southwestern tip of Saudi Arabia and Israel west across northern Africa from Egypt through Sudan, Libya, Tunisia, Algeria, Morocco, the Sahrawi Republic, Mauritania, Mali, and Niger. Hiding from the fierce desert sun by day, this nocturnal predator ambushes lizards and rodents by partially burying itself in the sand. It crawls via a sidewinding motion, and reproduces via eggs.

Introduction to Vipers

Terrestrial vipers and pitvipers can be found throughout the world in tropical and temperate zones, with the exception of Australia and New Guinea and a number of islands. This group includes tiny snakes like the Namaqua Dwarf Adder of the southern Namib region in Africa, a creature scarcely one foot long, to behemoths like the Amazon Bushmaster, which can exceed ten feet.

Vipers are of major medical importance. Investigation of their complex venoms has gleaned information of benefit in disease treatment, and some important inventions such as the hypodermic syringe and the heat-seeking missile derive from fangs and thermoreceptive pits, both features common to vipers.

Many kinds of vipers and pitvipers in the world's tropical forests have become specialized for life in the trees. They possess prehensile tails, compressed bodies to aid in climbing, and often are cryptically colored, resembling green vegetation or colorful leaves. All bear long fangs for effective capture and envenomation of prey, usually birds or lizards. Unlike most terrestrial vipers, those living in the trees tend to strike and retain their grip so as not to lose the food item. Perhaps this is why they tend to have large heads. Most arboreal vipers bear their young live, and the young of many species are born with a yellow or greenish tail-tip that may serve as a lure.

BK

Great Lakes Bush Viper *Atheris nitschei nitschei*

This heavy-bodied, 29-inch viper is semi-arboreal, basking in bushes but often hunting on the ground. This African species is found in Uganda, northwest Tanzania, Rwanda, Burundi, and Zaire. It occupies montane forest, elephant grass, and upland swamps. Preferred food items include rodents, lizards, and frogs.

95

Green Bush Viper

Atheris squamiger ssp.

This graceful snake, up to 30 inches in length and the largest of the bush vipers, shares a trait with only six other kinds of viper in its native Africa: arboreality (tree-dwelling). Its name refers to the most common color phase (as shown at right), but orange (as seen above), red, brown, and even blue specimens have been found. The bristly scales give this rather calm snake a particularly menacing appearance.

Widely distributed in rainforests of West and Central Africa, this nocturnal snake has been found up to 20 feet above the ground in vegetation, where it hunts for rodents, amphibians, lizards, and snakes. Seven to nine babies are born in March or April. Pugnacious, the Green Bush Viper defends itself readily, and it has been known to cause human fatality.

96

Wagler's Viper *Tropidolaemus wagleri*

With its exceptionally broad head and slender neck, this colorful snake looks, to some, like evil incarnate. But its dramatic build belies a generally even temperament. In fact, the Wagler's Viper is so sluggish that it is sometimes difficult to awaken. One Chinese temple in Penang, Malaysia, has become world famous because of the large numbers of this snake, also known as the Temple Viper, which festoon the statues and architecture. These individuals are so docile that visitors frequently handle them with impunity. The complex pattern and colors are subject to geographical variation, and many isolated island populations differ dramatically from those on the mainland. The range includes much of southeast Asia, from Thailand and Malaysia through Indonesia to the Philippines. Young, born in clutches of 10 to 20, are primarily green at birth, and the males, small at maturity, tend to resemble the juveniles. The much larger females undergo considerable change as they mature. Diet consists of birds, mammals, reptiles, and amphibians.

WL

Philippine Pitviper

Trimeresurus flavomaculatus flavomaculatus

Found only in the Philippine Archipelago, where it is widespread, this snake lives in humid tropical forest. Because the Philippines consists of over 7,000 islands, the many populations of this snake differ widely in color, pattern, food and habitat preferences. Reaching lengths in excess of five feet, these snakes feed on birds, amphibians, reptiles, and mammals.

McGregor's Pitviper

Trimeresurus flavomaculatus mcgregori

A race of the Philippine Pitviper, this beautiful reptile is restricted to Bataan Island. There, it can be found in a broad array of colors, ranging from yellow to silver or nearly white. McGregor's Pitviper averages about three feet in length. It feeds on a variety of amphibians, birds, lizards, and small mammals.

PC

White-lipped Tree Viper
Trimeresurus albolabris albolabris

There are several arboreal, green pitvipers in Southeast Asia, and all of them are superficially similar. The White-lipped Tree Viper is one of the most widespread, ranging in tropical lowland forests from northern India, Nepal, Myanmar (Burma), Thailand, Kampuchea, Laos, Vietnam, and southern China, through Hong Kong, West Malaysia, and part of Indonesia. Averaging about two feet in length, these snakes have caused numerous bites to humans. However, their venom is mild, fatalities are rare, and they are undeserving of the sinister reputation accorded them by the US soldiers who fought in Vietnam. The Viet Cong suspended these snakes at their tunnel entrances to strike fear in the hearts of the "tunnel rats" whose duty it was to clear the tunnels. As their legend grew, these American soldiers called them "two-steppers," because, supposedly, a victim of their bite would be dead by the time he took two steps.

Sri Lankan Pitviper
Trimeresurus trigonocephalus

This 30-inch snake is the only arboreal viper found on Sri Lanka (Ceylon), where it makes its home in forests, bamboo thickets, and along brushy streams. It is most commonly encountered in the humid tropical zone, and it has been found in spice plantations. Food consists of amphibians, birds, lizards, and small mammals. The young are born alive, and litters can contain as many as 26.

Eyelash Palm Pitviper *Bothriechis schlegelii*

So named because of the bristling scales over each eye, this two-foot serpent ranges from southern Mexico through Central America to Colombia, Venezuela, Ecuador, and northern Peru in South America. It lives in humid forests at low to intermediate elevations. Extraordinarily variable in color and pattern, the Eyelash Palm Pitviper can be brown, green, or pink, often with multicolored patterns of great complexity (as seen in the photo, below right). There is even a yellow phase (as seen in the photos above, and below, left). Newborn specimens feed on frogs and small lizards, while adults tend to prefer mammals and birds.

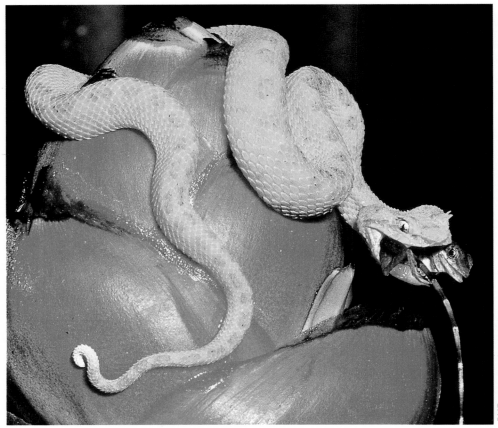

A yellow morph of the Eyelash Palm Pitviper eating an anole on a heliconia.

An Eyelash Palm Pitviper (*Bothriechis schlegelii*) on a palm leaf over a stream, showing a typical habitat.

Speckled Forest Pitviper

Bothriopsis taeniata taeniata

Because of its color and pattern, this snake blends in well with the foliage in the trees where it makes its home. As a result, it is seldom seen by local inhabitants. This five-foot pitviper is found throughout the Amazon and southern Orinocoan Basins of South America. Its habits are poorly known, but it feeds on marsupials (opossums) and rodents. This species is remarkable because of its extraordinarily long fangs.

Borneo Short-tailed Python
Python curtus breitensteini

This race of Blood Python is found in Indonesia on Kalimantan, in East Malaysia, and Singapore. Blood Pythons are proportionately the stoutest of the pythons. These stocky snakes may reach nine feet in length, but four to five feet is the norm. Some races are bright reddish-orange in coloration, presumably giving rise to the name. Ranging from Thailand and Malaysia through parts of Indonesia, Singapore, and Vietnam, the Blood Python is an inhabitant of freshwater marshes, swamps, and tropical wet forests. It primarily lives in the lowlands, where it is never far from moist habitat. Blood Pythons are all ambush predators, capturing mammals and birds with a lightning-like strike and overcoming them via constriction. Any mammal that can be constricted and consumed is potential prey, but cane rats are preferred. Females incubate their eggs within their coils.

Diamond Python *Morelia spilota spilota*

This distinctive snake is found in temperate southeastern Australia. It averages about six feet in length and often appears in residential neighborhoods while searching for bird and mammal prey, but is not a threat to humans. It is part of a group known as Carpet Pythons.

PC

Burmese Python *Python molurus bivittatus*

A snake of the Indian subcontinent and adjacent southern China, this is a race of the Indian Rock Python. Large and heavy-bodied, the Burmese Python may reach lengths in excess of 20 feet, but sexual maturity occurs at much smaller sizes. Females coil about their egg clutches, incubating them via "shivering," muscular contractions that produce heat. Clutches vary from 25 to 80 eggs, which hatch after two months. This species is remarkably hardy and remains common in many areas despite years of persecution for meat, hides, and the pet trade.

PC

Ball Python *Python regius*

Maturing at about three feet, Ball (or Royal) Pythons are among the smallest of their clan. They are abundant in the savanna and open woodland of west and central Africa. Secretive and nocturnal, Ball Pythons sometimes roll into a sphere, hiding their head within their powerful coils in order to protect themselves. They feed upon rodents, and the females produce from two to eight large eggs.

PMF

Centralian Carpet Python *Morelia bredli*

This relative of the Australian Carpet Python is native only to arid regions in the Northern Territory of Australia. Known to reach lengths in excess of eight feet, this powerful constrictor makes its home in crevices, small caves, and hollow trees in Red Gum forests and along waterways in desert. Its diet consists of birds and small mammals. Clutches of up to 47 eggs have been documented for this species.

Jungle Carpet Python
Morelia spilota cheynei

This is a race of the Diamond Python (page 102). It is found only along riverine gallery forests draining the Atherton Tablelands in northeastern Australia. Reaching about six feet in length, the Jungle Carpet Python prowls through wet subtropical forest and brush in search of small vertebrates on which it preys. Because of extensive habitat alteration due to logging and agriculture, this beautiful snake has a restricted range, and it may be vulnerable to extinction.

PC

Woma *Aspidites ramsayi*

This seven-and-one-half-foot python lives in Australia's dry interior and western regions where it favors scrub, grassland, and black-soil plains. It frequents rodent burrows and is a powerful excavator of soil. Its diet consists of mammals, birds, and reptiles. Female Womas lay from four to eight large eggs.

Calabar Burrowing Boa

Charina (Calabaria) reinhardtii

This odd, three-foot boa is distantly related to Rubber and Rosy Boas of North America. Adapted to life in the moist leaf litter of rainforests, this West African snake ranges from Liberia and Cameroon through Gabon, the Congo, and Zaire. When threatened, these gentle constrictors defend themselves by rolling into a tight ball with the head at the center. They eat small rodents and other vertebrates. The colors of this specimen are somewhat dull because it is almost ready to shed its skin.

Green Tree Python   *Morelia viridis*

Famed for its superficial resemblance to the Emerald Tree Boa of South America, this attractive six-foot denizen of Indonesian and northern Australian rainforests is a familiar zoo animal throughout the world. Yellow or rust-to-red colored at birth, the babies gradually become green or blue as they mature, and their color helps them blend with their lush surroundings. Sedentary by day, the Green Tree Python hunts at night for mammals, birds, and reptiles on which it feeds.

Above, the python's pupil is a vertical slit. But there is also a dark horizontal band crossing the eye. The resulting "+" shape is disruptive coloration which helps camouflage the eye. The honeycomb-like, pitted area around the mouth houses heat sensors for locating warm-blooded prey in the dark. Below, a red, immature Green Tree Python, feeds on a wild mouse.

This photo shows the mixed colors of a Green Tree Python in a transitional stage, as it changes from juvenile to adult.

Above, a typical, adult Green Tree Python. Note the blue stripes on this specimen.

Pythons and Boas

A single family, the Boidae, unites snakes belonging to five groups, or subfamilies. Most conspicuous among these are the pythons (Pythoninae) and boas (Boinae). Many species are large and colorful. These very powerful constrictors have inspired tales of terror spanning the centuries. Most boas and pythons are tropical, and they superficially resemble one another. However, there are fundamental differences between the groups. Most boas, for instance, are live-bearers, while pythons lay eggs. Within these two groups are found both arboreal and terrestrial snakes, and sizes may range from three feet to over 20. These sometimes giant snakes have long been persecuted for their hides and meat, for the live animal trade, and as objects of misguided revulsion. Today, many species are bred in captivity.

Above, a blue-phase adult

Ringed Python *Bothrochilus boa*

Confined to one of the world's exotic corners, this sleek predator is common-to-abundant over portions of Papua, New Guinea, and the volcanic islands of the Bismarck Archipelago. Ringed Pythons are lithe, six-foot constrictors which begin life cloaked in tawny orange and black, but the color fades to bronze with age. This snake is an opportunist, feeding on a variety of small vertebrates and occupying a variety of habitats. It is likely that the young derive benefit from their resemblance to one of the region's venomous species, the Banded Small-eyed Snake, *Loveridgelaps elapoides*.

Reticulated Python *Python reticulata*

Perhaps the longest snake in the world, this python may attain truly gigantic proportions, and reports of lengths in excess of 30 feet seem reliable. Such specimens are exceedingly rare, however, and sexual maturity may be attained at 12 feet. Reticulated Pythons are found from the Philippines westward throughout southeast Asia, including many islands. An inhabitant of lowland tropical forest, this species often wanders into habitations and agricultural areas when foraging. Large adults can overcome prey as large as as pigs or deer and, very rarely, humans. Clutches of up to several dozen eggs are laid. The emergent juveniles measure as much as 30 inches. This species has long been persecuted for its hide and for the pet trade.

Arizona Mountain Kingsnake
Lampropeltis pyromelana pyromelana

For varieties of mountain kingsnakes, the isolated mountain ranges of the southwestern US and northern Mexico are veritable islands in an arid sea. Trapped for eons within each range, the mountain kingsnakes evolved into spectacular varieties, distinct in each area. Occupants of wooded streamsides, these harmless, 30-inch snakes survive on a diet of lizards and small rodents. Like other members of the kingsnake clan, they are egg-laying constrictors.

Scarlet Kingsnake *Lampropeltis triangulum elapsoides*

One of the smallest and most attractive of the so-called "milksnakes," the Scarlet Kingsnake seldom exceeds 24 inches in length. A native of the southeastern United States, this species typically lives in pine flatwoods, where much of its time is spent secretively beneath logs or forest debris. Skinks form the major part of the diet, although larger specimens consume small rodents. The term "milksnake" derives from the mistaken belief that these animals enter barns in order to suck milk from cows. Of course, the attraction would be rodents rather than milk, and no snake possesses the ability to extract milk from a cow.

California Kingsnake
Lampropeltis getula californiae

Beautifully ringed or striped, this powerful constrictor ranges over much of the western US and adjacent northwest Mexico. In general, kingsnakes are active during the early morning and twilight hours, when they cruise about in search of reptiles, amphibians, birds, eggs, and small mammals upon which they prey. Averaging about three feet in length, California Kingsnakes were long thought to represent two different species, one ringed and the other striped. However, it was eventually shown that both patterns can be present in a single clutch of babies.

At right, the "Desert Phase" of the California Kingsnake.

"Blotched" Kingsnake
Lampropeltis getula getula X L.g. floridana

Native to the Florida panhandle region, this distinctive population of the Common Kingsnake comes from a zone in which two races overlap (intergrade). Specimens from this area may be striped, banded, or even patternless. Typically, such a specimen has a blotched appearance, and the juveniles often bear reddish coloration on their sides. Blotched Kings are considerably smaller than their relatives to the north and south, and seldom exceed four feet in length. The specimen shown here is a young snake with an unusual color.

PC

Gray-banded Kingsnake *Lampropeltis alterna*

This handsome, three-foot snake is primarily a resident of the Chihuahuan Desert. It ranges in the US from Trans-Pecos Texas and southeastern New Mexico eastward to Edwards County, Texas, and south into Mexico (in Durango and Nuevo León). Primarily nocturnal, the Gray-banded Kingsnake (or Blair's Kingsnake) forages along rocky canyon walls and outcrops for diurnal lizards, which it captures while they sleep. Its habitat consists of limestone and granite outcrops with deep crevices and caprocks. Variable in pattern and color, this snake has long been prized by collectors and professional breeders.

"Variable" Kingsnake

Lampropeltis mexicana

This population, also known as Thayer's Kingsnake, is aptly named. Snakes born in the same litter often bear little resemblance to one another, some being beige with reddish dorsal saddles, and others ringed in black, red, and white. Found in Tamaulipas in northeast Mexico, these snakes reach about three feet in length.

PC

111

Honduran Milksnake *Lampropeltis triangulum hondurensis*

Just as the Viceroy Butterfly benefits from its resemblance to the toxic Monarch, so do the milksnakes, which look remarkably like venomous coralsnakes. A native of Honduras and adjacent regions, this beautiful and harmless species can exceed six feet in length, making it one of the largest of the · milksnakes. In the Sula Plain of Honduras, several kinds of snakes exhibit a "tangerine" coloration (as shown above), including the local coralsnake. Not surprisingly, the Honduran Milksnake from that region is orange as well. Five to ten eggs make up a typical clutch. ·

The photo at left shows the typical coloration of the harmless Honduran Milksnake. Note its remarkable resemblance to a deadly coralsnake, a likeness which gives it a certain amount of protection.

Eastern Milksnake *Lampropeltis triangulum triangulum*

A diverse group of kingsnakes, similar largely because they tend to be boldly ringed in bright colors, ranges collectively from Canada to southern Ecuador and western Venezuela. They are known as milksnakes, a colloquialism stemming from the myth that one of them, the Eastern Milksnake, frequents barns in order to suck milk from the cows. A bit less gaily-colored than its relatives, the Eastern Milksnake is none-the-less handsome, reaching three to four feet in length and occupying stone piles, old fields, woodland and, yes, barnyards, throughout the northeastern US and adjacent Canada. Like all kingsnakes it is a powerful constrictor, and it preys on small rodents and reptiles. Eggs are deposited in the spring inside decaying logs and similar sites.

Pueblan Milksnake

Lampropeltis triangulum campbelli

It seems amazing that so imposing a reptile might have gone unnoticed by science until the 1980's, but that is precisely the case with this four-foot native of the deserts of central Mexico. Adapted to the rigors of a harsh environment where rain may come once a year or not at all, this harmless and beautiful constrictor spends much of its time underground in burrows, where it searches for lizard and small mammal prey.

Amazon Tree Boa
Corallus hortulanus

One of the most variable of snakes, this slender, arboreal species may be brown and silver, red, or even yellow. Some specimens possess bold patterns while others are unmarked. Adept at climbing, this nonvenomous snake has long, fang-like teeth to assist it in capturing the birds, mammals, and lizards on which it feeds. Like all members of the boa family, the Amazon Tree Boa relies on constriction to subdue its prey. Up to 12 or more young are born alive after a gestation period of several months. A broad variety of patterns and colors may be represented within a single litter. This species lives in humid lowland forest throughout the Amazon and part of the Orinocoan Basins of South America.

This Amazon Tree Boa is coiling in preparation for a strike.

Above, two Amazon Tree Boas show how variable the colors of this species can be.

Kenya Sand Boa *Eryx colubrinus loveridgei*

With eyes situated practically on top of its head, tiny nostrils, and tightly overlapping scales, the Kenya Sand Boa is supremely adapted for life in the arid, sandy regions of east Africa. Whether gliding gracefully under the surface of desert soils or lying in ambush with only its snout and eyes exposed, Sand Boas are masters at avoiding detection. Short and stocky, this species seldom exceeds 24 inches in length. Lizards and small rodents are their prey.

Coastal Rosy Boa *Charina (Lichanura) trivirgata roseofusca*

Attractive, docile, and scarcely reaching 40 inches in length, the Rosy Boa of southwestern North America has long been popular as a pet. Fortunately, throughout much of its range, this beautiful snake is protected. This smooth-scaled constrictor prefers rocky hillsides where it emerges by night from crevices to hunt for small rodents. There are several distinctive races of this snake. Rosy Boas are known to have lived for 18 years or more in captivity.

Emerald Tree Boa
Corallus caninus

Populations of this beautiful arboreal snake are found in humid forest across northern South America. There is some geographical variation, and Amazon specimens often possess more white dorsal markings than do their relatives from the Guianas. These snakes are extremely sluggish, often occupying a single branch in their treetop homes for many weeks. They feed on birds and mammals. Emerald Tree Boa babies are usually red or rust-colored at birth, undergoing a dramatic transformation as they mature, until their overall color is a glistening forest-green. The Emerald Tree Boa at left is a juvenile born to a green-colored mother from the wild and illustrates this dramatic color change when compared to the adult at top.

Common Rainbow Boa *Epicrates cenchria cenchria*

This attractive relative of the Anaconda ranges from southern Costa Rica south to Bolivia. There are a number of distinctive races. The specimen pictured here is often, and mistakenly, called the Brazilian Rainbow Boa. While much of its range indeed lies within Brazil, so do the ranges of at least six other races of rainbow boa. The Common Rainbow Boa is found throughout the Amazon and southern Orinocoan Basins of equatorial South America, east of the Andes mountains.

Averaging four to six feet in length, these constrictors are so named because they have a purplish iridescence when exposed to strong light. Like most boas, this species is nocturnal, using its vision and heat-sensitive labial pits to locate birds, lizards, and rodents in primary forest where it lives. Rainbow boas live near water. They have been found submerged in streams, and prowling inside caves hunting bats. The young are born alive and are less colorful than the adults.

Cuban Dwarf Boa

Tropidophis melanurus melanurus

This three-foot, terrestrial boa is native to Cuba, where it occupies a variety of habitats including forest, drier, rocky regions, and agricultural clearings. Nocturnal, the Cuban Dwarf Boa uses its constricting coils to subdue amphibians, lizards, birds and rodents. Females produce about eight young in August and September, when *Anolis* lizards, an important prey item, are abundant. This species varies in color from brown to tan, gray, or reddish. The specimen shown here is the rare red phase.

117

Corn Snake *Elaphe guttata guttata*

Also known as the Red Rat Snake, this species, with its many color phases, is one of the most beautiful snakes in the United States. The specimen shown here is from Oketee, South Carolina. Seldom exceeding five feet in length, this constrictor gained its name because of its habit of frequenting corn cribs in search of rodent prey. Knowledgeable farmers appreciate this species for this reason. Females lay about 20 eggs in a clutch, usually in late spring or early summer.

Royal Diadem Snake

Spalerosophis diadema diadema

These snakes are large (up to seven feet), robust, and imposing. They are important consumers of rodents throughout their range. Inhabitants of rocky regions in arid or semi-arid regions from western India to Pakistan, Royal Diadem Snakes hunt for prey in crevices or even up in trees. When confronted, this species hisses loudly and defends itself vigorously. Variable throughout its range in color and pattern, there is disagreement as to whether one or several species are represented.

Mandarin Rat Snake *Elaphe mandarina*

As ornately colored as its name implies, this snake is found at intermediate and high elevations from India and Myanmar (Burma) through Vietnam to China and Taiwan. Reaching lengths in excess of five feet, but commonly much smaller, the Mandarin Ratsnake is a denizen of open mountain forests and rocky areas. It is frequently encountered in agricultural areas. A secretive species, this snake spends much of its time foraging for rodents within their burrows. Males are known to engage in ritual combat as part of their mating behavior. Females produce three to eight eggs.

Trans-Pecos Rat Snake

Bogertophis subocularis

The lovely pastels of the Chihuahuan Desert are reflected in the subtle hues of this secretive predator. Found in desert regions of west Texas, southeast New Mexico, and adjacent Mexico, the Trans-Pecos Rat Snake takes shelter by day in rock piles and rodent burrows. In the cool of the evening it emerges to hunt for rodents, bats, and birds. Its large protruding eyes aid it during its nocturnal forays. Up to five feet in length, this harmless constrictor lays three to seven eggs during the summer. There is a species of tick which is unique to this snake; specimens often lose the tip of their tail due to wounds produced when this tick attaches itself.

Red-tailed Ratsnake *Gonyosoma oxycephalum*
Powerful, arboreal constrictors, Red-tailed Ratsnakes reach lengths of over seven feet. They are found in lowland rain forests across southeast Asia in Indonesia, Cambodia, India (Andaman and Nicobar Islands), Laos, Myanmar (Burma), Malaysia, the Philippines, Singapore, Thailand, and Vietnam. Juveniles feed on lizards while adults are mammal specialists, feeding on bats and rodents. This sleek egg-layer inflates itself and displays its striking blue tongue when threatened. Color varies in this species according to the island on which it occurs. For example, this specimen of Red-tailed Ratsnake has a gray tail rather than the usual pink.

Cave Ratsnake *Elaphe taeniura ridleyi*
A denizen of wooded hills on the Malaysian Peninsula, this species occurs from southern Thailand south through Malaysia. Up to seven feet or more in length, this slender constrictor frequents caves and crevices in the limestone hills where it feeds on bats and other mammals. However, it is also found in rain forest, and occasionally around human settlements.

Striped Keelback
Xenochrophis vittatus

A slender, two-foot frog-eater, the Striped Keelback favors marshes and other wet areas in Indonesia (Bangka, Java, Sumatra), and Singapore, where an introduced population is thriving. When threat-ened, this snake enters the water and swims away rapidly. This species is abundant on Java and appears to be increasing in Singapore.

Garter Snakes *Thamnophis sp.*

The thirty or so species of the genus *Thamnophis* probably include the most commonly encountered and widespread of North America's snakes. Not surprisingly, they have been the object of much research. Garter snakes range from Canada south to central Costa Rica, and from sea-level to 6000 feet in the mountains, favoring swampy locales where their favorite prey, amphibians, worms, or fishes, can best be located. Most species are smaller than three feet in length, although some grow larger, and one species is known to exceed five feet. Most have a striped pattern and are adept at fleeing when alarmed. Like their relatives the water snakes, most garters will bite and produce an unpleasant musk if restrained. Females give birth to as many as 30 offspring or more.

Red-sided Garter Snake *Thamnophis sirtalis parietalis*

One of eleven races of the wide-ranging Common Garter Snake, the Red-sided is found from the Red River Valley throughout the Great Plains of the US northward in Canada as far as the Northwest Territories. It is the most northerly distributed snake in the Western Hemisphere. The distinctive red or orange bars in the dorsal pattern give this snake its name. It is a denizen of waterways where it hunts for its amphibian prey. Up to four feet in length, but averaging much smaller, this snake is commonly encountered in the eastern part of its range.

121

San Francisco Garter Snake *Thamnophis sirtalis tetrataenia*

This species shares its entire range with the burgeoning metropolis of San Francisco. Trapped on the peninsula, its numbers are dwindling, and this garter snake population has been accorded Endangered status and enjoys heavy protection.

Captive breeding for release might substantially benefit this race. Considered by many to be the most beautiful of the garter snakes, this inoffensive species feeds on earthworms, fish, and frogs, gives birth to live young, and, like most garter snakes, frequents moist areas. It seldom exceeds 30 inches in length.

Northern Checkered Garter Snake
Thamnophis marcianus marcianus

This robust, three-foot snake ranges from Kansas and southeastern California in the US southward in northern and eastern Mexico to northern Veracruz. It is an occupant of arid grasslands and deserts, always near a water source, from lowlands to 5300 feet above sea-level. In some areas, this species is primarily terrestrial, while in places like Arizona it is known to be semiaquatic. Primarily diurnal, Checkered Garter Snakes forage for fishes, earthworms and amphibians, the latter being preferred. Females may produce up to 31 offspring.

Plains Garter Snake

Thamnophis radix

Found in wet prairies from Alberta, Canada, and Montana southeastward to Ohio and north Texas, this three-foot reptile consumes a wide variety of prey, from leeches and earthworms, to fish, rodents, and amphibians. In contrast to most snakes, which tend to occur individually, Plains Garter Snakes reach very high densities, and as many as 845 have been recorded in one hectare of land. Populations in Manitoba, Canada, produce on average 30 offspring per clutch.

Red-spotted Garter Snake *Thamnophis sirtalis concinnus*

Another attractive race of the ubiquitous Common Garter Snake, the Red-spotted Garter Snake is found along the Pacific coast of the US from the Olympic Peninsula south to the vicinity of San Diego, California.

BL

Eastern Diamondback Rattlesnake *Crotalus adamanteus*

Largest of all rattlesnakes, this magnificent creature ranks as one of the biggest venomous snakes in the world. Known to have reached eight feet in length and weigh in excess of 25 pounds, today this species no longer reaches such dimensions. Diamondbacks reside in sparsely populated stretches of palmetto and turkey oak forest or pine flatlands in the southeastern US.

Above, a leucistic Eastern Diamondback Rattlesnake.

Habitat destruction and persecution for hides and meat have combined to drastically reduce populations of this snake. Large adults prefer cottontail rabbits as prey, but any small mammal may be accepted. Due to its size and potent venom, the Eastern Diamondback is a dangerous snake, and bites to humans can be fatal. Offspring can measure as much as 15 inches at birth.

PC

Carolina Pigmy Rattlesnake
Sistrurus miliarius miliarius

At two feet in length, the Carolina Pigmy is one of the most diminutive of rattlesnakes. It is a denizen of pine-oak scrub and pine flatwoods of the Atlantic coastal plain from the Carolinas through Georgia to Alabama. Populations also exist in the interior piedmont. The coloration of this species varies according to locality, with specimens from the extreme northeast of the range, in North Carolina's Albemarle-Pamlico Sound Peninsula being notable for their reddish to pinkish dorsal ground color. Active by day and by night, the Carolina Pigmy hunts for frogs, small reptiles, and mammals. In August or September, females give birth to three to nine babies.

Mottled Rock Rattlesnake *Crotalus lepidus lepidus*

One of four races of the Rock Rattlesnake, this small reptile lives in a variety of habitats in southeastern New Mexico and southwestern Texas in the US, and south across much of the eastern Mexican plateau. Reaching 30 inches in length but averaging much smaller, the Mottled Rock Rattlesnake lives in pine-oak forests, mesquite grassland, and Chihuahuan Desert. Alert and secretive, this species preys primarily on lizards and small rodents, and is active mostly by day

Introduction to Rattlesnakes *Crotalus* and *Sistrurus*

Among the world's most awe-inspiring reptiles, one must count the venomous rattlesnakes, which range collectively from Canada south to Argentina, practically the entire Western Hemisphere. Aptly named because of their distinctive tail appendage, the rattle, these conspicuous snakes have long played a role in folklore and human culture. Rattlesnakes have inspired fear, reverence, and wildly exaggerated tales. They have also been important in medicinal applications and as sources of food or hides.

Some species possess virulent venoms, and all rattlesnakes may be termed dangerously venomous. Toxicological studies on the pharmacological effects of rattlesnake venoms are an important branch of biomedical research. In parts of the US the rattlesnake is "hunted" as a source of recreation and revenue in so-called "roundups." These are especially prevalent in Texas, Oklahoma, and Alabama, and they have proven to be both popular and controversial.

Like all pitvipers, rattlesnakes possess a facial orifice which aids in heat and/or infrared detection, providing the snake with information that could aid in defense or predation. The distinctive rattle, presumably used as a warning device, consists of brittle, horny segments that are added each time the snake sheds its skin. These structures break frequently and in no way indicate the age of the serpent.

Most rattlesnakes are members of the genus *Crotalus*, although three species possessing distinctive enlarged plates on the top of the head are grouped in the genus *Sistrurus*, often called Pigmy Rattlers. The rattlesnakes include 29 species that range in size from two feet to the spectacularly impressive, eight-foot Eastern Diamondback, one of the largest venomous reptiles in the world.

Rattlesnakes exist in myriad habitats, including desert, chapparral, lowland swamp forest, prairies, alpine and cloud forests, and mountain plateaus. They occur from sea-level to over 14,000 feet in the mountains. All are live-bearers, and prey includes mammals, birds, reptiles, amphibians, and the occasional invertebrate.

Mexican Rattlesnake
Crotalus durissus culminatus

This race of the widespread Neotropical Rattlesnake is found in the coastal lowlands and foothills of Mexico's west coast, from Michoacan south to the Isthmus of Tehuantepec. An inhabitant of rugged thornscrub and coastal dry forest, this rattlesnake normally looks like the specimen pictured above. The specimen at right is xanthic, a genetic condition in which yellow pigments in the skin predominate. The normal specimen at the top of the page is preparing to shed its skin, and this will peel off in a single piece. Prior to this happening, however, fluids are secreted beneath the old layer, and they often are visible as a milky or bluish color seen over the eye.

Uracoan Rattlesnake *Crotalus durissus vegrandis*

One of 14 races of the Neotropical Rattlesnake (*Crotalus durissus*), most widely distributed of all rattlesnakes, this reptile is native to the Maturín savanna region in Venezuela. Unlike most of its close relatives, the Uracoan Rattlesnake is pallid gray and often heavily speckled dorsally. While specimens encountered in the wild tend to be rather small, captives attain sizes in excess of four feet. The venom is extremely toxic and aids in subduing the rodents upon which the Uracoan Rattlesnake preys.

Chihuahuan Ridgenose Rattlesnake
Crotalus willardi silus

This rattlesnake barely exceeds 24 inches in length. It lives in pine-oak woodland, oak scrub, and open, grassy meadows, usually favoring wetter areas, at elevations up to 9,000 feet above sea-level. The range includes the states of Sonora and Chihuahua in Mexico in the Sierra Madre Occidental and isolated smaller ranges of mountains. Its diet includes small birds and mammals, as well as lizards, centipedes, and scorpions.

Canebrake Rattlesnake
Crotalus horridus atricaudatus

Considered by some to be a single race, the Timber Rattlesnake, the populations found in the lowlands of the southeastern US from coastal Virginia to eastern Texas are distinctive in structure, coloration, and ecology. Reaching six feet in length, this occupant of swamps, cane thickets, and hardwood bottomlands is a predator on squirrels. Females can reproduce at the age of six, and give birth to six to ten young from July to September. Due to loss of habitat, this snake is now protected in many parts of its range.

PC

Blacktail Rattlesnake *Crotalus molossus molossus*

Reaching about four feet in length, this beautiful species is found from Texas to Arizona in the US, south into most of northern Mexico and on Isla Tiburón. The Blacktail Rattlesnake frequents upland habitats such as stream beds, talus slopes, coniferous forests, rocky arroyos, and desert flats, from about 1,000 to over 3,000 feet above sea-level. Adults tend to be mild-mannered, seasonally nocturnal, and feed on mammals and birds. About seven young are born in July or August and they include lizards in their diet. The overall color varies geographically, with eastern populations tending to be greenish gray while western populations are sometimes strikingly yellow or orange, and black.

Southwestern Speckled Rattlesnake

Crotalus mitchellii pyrrhus

There are five races recognized of this three-foot snake, and collectively they occupy dry, rocky regions from southern Nevada and Utah south through California and Arizona in the US, and continuing into Mexico in Sonora and the Baja California Peninsula. Several islands in the Gulf of California and one in the Pacific are also inhabited by this species. The vertical range is to over 8,000 feet above sea-level. Speckled Rattlesnakes hide in crevices during the heat of the day, emerging later to hunt for the mammals and birds on which they prey. Females produce up to 11 offspring between July and September.

PC

Gloyd's Cantil
Agkistrodon bilineatus howardgloydi

Southernmost of the four races of Cantil, this stunning three-foot reptile occupies dry forest and coastal thornscrub along the Pacific coast of Honduras, Nicaragua, and Costa Rica. Cantils are able to withstand arid conditions by hiding in crevices. They emerge after rains and prowl about in search of frogs and other small vertebrates. Cantils have a highly toxic venom. The name, Cantil, derives from the Tzeltal Indian name, *kantiil*, which means, "yellow lips."

Broad-banded Copperhead *Agkistrodon contortrix laticinctus*
This is one of five races of Copperhead in North America. This three-foot pitviper ranges through scrub oak and gallery forest in central Texas and Oklahoma north to southern Kansas.

Florida Cottonmouth (juvenile)
Agkistrodon piscivorous conanti

There are three races of this robust pitviper, and they range collectively across the southeastern portion of the US. Cottonmouths are semi-aquatic, favoring sloughs, swamps, and bayous. Their diet includes amphibians, fishes, reptiles, and small mammals, but this species will consume just about anything it can capture. The subject of much speculation and superstition, Cottonmouths are regularly confused with harmless watersnakes. Note the yellow tail which is used as a lure for frogs.

KS

Puff Adder *Bitis arietans arietans*

Like its cousin the Gaboon Adder, this is a large and heavy, venomous snake. It is one of the most significant sources of venomous human snakebite throughout its range in the drier portions of sub-Saharan Africa. Occasional individuals may exceed six feet in length, but this species averages about half that size. Mainly terrestrial and basically nocturnal, this sluggish snake relies on its coloration to enable it to escape detection. When confronted, the Puff Adder will exhale noisily, hence its common name. This species prefers open grassy regions, where it feeds on small rodents and just about any other vertebrate of suitable size. Females are live-bearers, and a litter of 156, the largest known for any snake, has been recorded. The specimen shown above is unusual because it is striped rather than blotched.

PMF

Peringuey's Adder *Bitis peringueyi*

This diminutive, foot-long viper is a native of the Namib Desert of Namibia and Angola, in southern Africa. Sidewinding from dune to dune across the sands, these snakes easily bury themselves as a means of hiding and heat avoidance. Peringuey's Adder is a live-bearer, giving birth to four to ten young. Lizards comprise its diet.

Desert Death Adder
Acanthophis pyrrhus

Death Adders look remarkably like vipers, although they actually belong to the family Elapidae, just like cobras and coralsnakes. Native to arid central Australia, the two-foot Desert Death Adder possesses raised and keeled head shields and heavily keeled body scales. Shy and sluggish, Death Adders usually attempt to hide in leaf litter when approached. However, they are capable of striking with great speed, and their potent venom has caused human fatalities. Rodents and lizards make up their diet.

Langsdorff's Coralsnake *Micrurus langsdorffii*

One of the most unusual of the coralsnakes because of its highly variable color and pattern, this two-foot reptile is native to the northwest Amazon Basin in South America. All specimens tend to possess white and red or pink rings, but the other color may be yellow, brown, or nearly black. Langsdorff's Coralsnake feeds on small lizards and snakes which it subdues with its powerful venom.

Coralsnakes are beautiful, famed for their brilliant colors, possess potent venom, and belong to a family of snakes, the Elapidae, that is distributed everywhere but Europe. Like their cousins the cobras, mambas, and kraits, coralsnakes have short, permanently erect front fangs and a venom that acts primarily on the nervous system. They occupy diverse habitats. Most coralsnake species prey on snakes or lizards, but some feed on fishes or amphibians.

Elapid Snakes: Cobras, Coralsnakes, and their Kin

Venomous snakes with fixed (immovable) front fangs are united in a single family, the Elapidae (although some authorities disagree and separate the seasnakes). Worldwide in distribution, this group includes, among others, cobras and mambas, kraits, coralsnakes, and seasnakes. Most are possessed of potent venoms,

and the majority can inflict life-threatening bites. However, with some notable exceptions, most species are secretive and for this reason do not come into contact with humans. However, when bitten, the risk of fatality is high, especially from the bites of the cobra and krait species.

Northern Many-banded Coralsnake

Micrurus multifasciatus hertwigi

Slender, and over three feet long, this black-and-orange or black-and-white snake favors moist upland forests in its native Nicaragua, Costa Rica, and eastern Panama. Unlike most coral snake species, this reptile only possesses two colors rather than three. Secretive, it spends much of its time in leaf litter searching for caecilians and small reptiles which make up its diet.

Eastern Coralsnake

Micrurus fulvius fulvius

Although this, the most northern of the coral snakes, can reach four feet in length, it is more commonly about half that size. The Eastern Coralsnake is a denizen of lowland forests from North Carolina and Mississippi south to the coast. This venomous reptile feeds on lizards and especially snakes, which it quickly subdues with a powerful venom. Throughout its range, there are several harmless mimics from which the venomous Eastern Coralsnake can be distinguished by the fact that its red and yellow rings are always in contact. Coralsnakes are secretive, wandering on the surface only during periods of high humidity or at dawn and dusk. In spite of their potent venom, coralsnakes seldom inflict bites on humans.

Coral Neck-band Snake *Scaphiodontophis annulatus*

This snake looks like an unfinished painting, but in fact its pattern is useful. Spending much of the day lying in ambush among dead leaves on the rain forest floor, this lizard-hunter has its head and neck exposed. This renders it vulnerable to predators such as birds. So, the front end of the harmless Coral Neck-band Snake is patterned to resemble something dangerous, like a venomous coral snake, while the remainder of its body is designed to blend with leaves. Ranging from Mexico to western Colombia, this two-foot snake feeds on skinks.

Western Longnose Snake

Rhinocheilus lecontei lecontei

This attractive, 30-inch constrictor is found in the southwestern and south-central portions of the US and northern Mexico. It ranges from southwest Kansas south to Texas and west to California, primarily in the lowlands. Habitat with grassy vegetation and low bushes is preferred. Its diet primarily consists of lizards and small mammals. The Longnose Snake is an egg layer.

133

WL

Amazon Parrot Snake

Leptophis ahaetulla nigromarginata

Slender and agile tree climbers, Parrot Snakes are found from Mexico to Bolivia. Days are spent actively foraging for sleeping treefrogs, which constitute their preferred prey. Depending upon the species, maximum length may be as much as seven feet. Parrot Snakes are egg layers. Parrot Snakes do not possess venom, but humans have suffered unpleasant symptoms when bitten by Parrot Snakes. This may be due to toxic secretions from their amphibian prey.

PC

At left, a Parrot Snake (*Leptophis ahaetulla*) gaping defensively. This display makes the snake seem larger and might startle a predator. In the bottom of the snake's mouth there is an opening to the windpipe which allows the snake to breathe when upward pressure from prey being swallowed closes the normal airways.

Introduction to Gopher Snakes
Pituophis sp.

Powerful constrictors, Gopher Snakes feed on rodents, birds and their eggs, and occasionally lizards and insects. Hiding by day from the hot, dry climate in which they live, Gopher Snakes emerge at dusk from crevices and rodent burrows to hunt. These nonvenomous snakes deposit their eggs in spring or early summer, and they hatch in about two months.

Cape Gopher Snake
Pituophis catenifer vertebralis

This three- to four-foot constrictor makes its home in the rugged hills of lower Baja California, Mexico. Ranging through a diversity of habitats, this Gopher Snake seeks the birds and mammals that make up its diet. Gopher Snakes are active by day during certain times of the year, but in steamy Baja, this species is more apt to emerge from hiding during the cooler evening hours.

Pacific Gopher Snake
Pituophis catenifer catenifer
(Albino specimen with a striped pattern)

A denizen of rocky arroyos, sagebrush flats, and all kinds of woodland, this three-foot serpent makes its home in California and adjacent Oregon along the west coast of the US. Extensive captive breeding has promoted several unusual color morphs of this snake, and these probably should be recognized as domestic animals. In nature, the Pacific Gopher Snake possesses a blotched dorsal pattern. Rodents and birds comprise its diet.

135

Blunt-headed Tree Snake *Imantodes cenchoa*

This may be the most proportionately slender snake in the world. Reaching lengths of up to four feet, it appears to be half that size. Abundant in rainforest from Mexico south to Bolivia, this species gracefully prowls about at night in trees and shrubs, hunting for small lizards and frogs. Bulging eyes allow for efficient nocturnal vision. Although it possesses a mild venom, this inoffensive snake is not known to bite and is considered harmless to humans.

Mexican Hognose Snake *Heterodon nasicus kennerlyi*

This stocky little snake lives in dry, sandy prairies of southwestern US and parts of north and central Mexico. Hognose Snakes are named for their upturned snouts, which they use to pry toads out of their defensive positions (flat against the ground). A Hognose Snake, when threatened, pretends to strike. If this ruse fails, it rolls onto its back, writhes in agony, and feigns death. After a brief wait, the Hognose Snake crawls away.

Banded Hognose Snake *Lystrophis semicinctus*

This two-foot snake is a coralsnake mimic. That is, it looks and behaves like a venomous coralsnake (*Micrurus*) and presumably scares away potential predators by doing so. Found in seasonally dry areas of Bolivia, Paraguay, Argentina, Brazil, and Uruguay, this harmless snake feeds on toads and lizards.

Madagascar Leafnose Snake
Langaha madagascariensis

The bizarre nasal protrusion makes this one of the strangest looking snakes in the world. Distributed throughout Madagascar, the Leafnose Snake is a tree dweller. Its slender build, muted coloration, and habit of remaining stiffly motionless combine with its unusual snout to make this snake resemble a twig or branch, thus helping it to escape detection. Males are easily distinguishable from females: males are brown with a white stripe along the side, while females are soft gray with darker mottling and have the namesake, frilled nasal decorations. The Leafnose Snake forages actively by day in search of lizards and small rodents. Both male and female are well camouflaged as vines or tree branches.

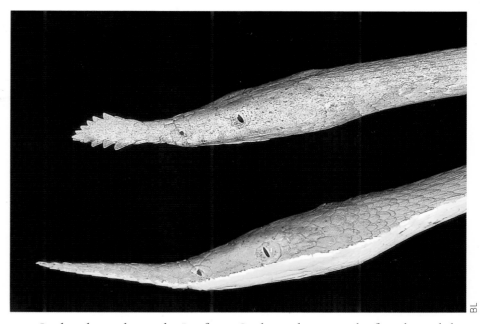

In the photo above, the Leafnose Snake at the top is the female, and the more colorful male is below. Note that the male has a sharply pointed snout.

Golden Tree Snake
Chrysopelea ornata ornatissima

Reaching nearly five feet in length, this attractive southeast Asian species is an adept and athletic tree climber. By coiling and suddenly straightening the body while flattening themselves, these snakes can glide for some distance through the air to escape predators. For this reason, these lizard-eaters are sometimes referred to as "flying snakes."

Sulawesi Mangrove Snake
Boiga dendrophila gemmicincta

The Mangrove Snake, wide-ranging throughout tropical southeast Asia, is comprised of several isolated island races. The Sulawesi Mangrove Snake is restricted to the archipelago of the same name (formerly known as Celebes). A large Mangrove Snake can exceed seven feet in length, and lengths of five to six feet are not uncommon. This voracious nocturnal predator makes its home in trees, including mangroves, where it hunts by night for a wide variety of birds, mammals, reptiles, amphibians, and even the occasional fish which make up its diet. This reptile is mildly venomous and possesses a pair of venom-conducting fangs, set at the rear of the mouth. It defends itself readily by flattening and raising its neck, gaping and biting, but its venom is too mild to pose a serious threat to humans. The adult is shown at right, the juvenile above.

Mangrove Snake *Boiga dendrophila dendrophila*

Possessing short, grooved, and relatively inefficient fangs in the rear of the mouth, this gaudy seven-to-eight-foot long snake hunts for bird, lizard, and mammal prey in the trees at night. Native to rainforests of southeast Asia, Indonesia, the Philippines, and Malaysia, it has been responsible for a few serious bites to humans (including the author!) but no fatalities. Two rear-fanged snakes from Africa, the Boomslang and the Twig Snake, are deadly, and each is responsible for the death of a prominent herpetologist.

Dog-tooth Catsnake *Boiga cynodon* (below)

All catsnakes possess vertically elliptical pupils and are arboreal. The Dog-tooth Catsnake, so named due to the enlarged teeth at the front of its mouth, is widely distributed in humid forests from Thailand and Malaysia through Indonesia and the Philippines. These gentle reptiles are nocturnal and feed primarily upon birds and their eggs. All catsnakes are egg-layers and all are mildly venomous, with a pair of fangs located at the rear of the mouth. A nearly black phase of this species is not uncommon in Malaysia and southern Thailand.

139

A snake charmer with a Common Cobra.

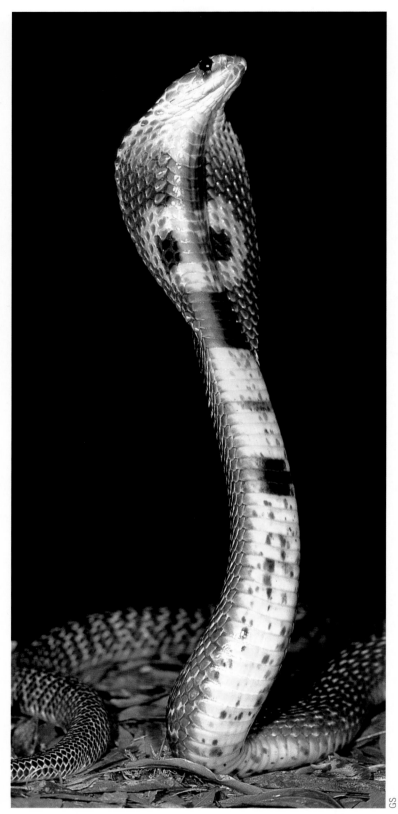

A Common Cobra shows the color inside its hood.

Common Cobra *Naja naja* •

A classically famous (or infamous) snake, the Common Cobra is found in a great variety of habitats from Pakistan, Nepal, and Bangladesh, south through India to Sri Lanka. The various populations exhibit quite an array of patterns and colors. Typically three to five feet in length, cobras frequently prowl about in search of frogs and other small vertebrates. The population inhabiting Pakistan is generally black in color. Snake charmers in the region have long taken advantage of this reptile's tendency to raise its ribs and spread its hood when alarmed, and its habit of swaying when confronted with a waving flute.

This has led many to believe these snakes can hear (they cannot) and are moving to the music. Common Cobras vary geographically in terms of their hood markings, a fact which has given rise to many names for different races. In addition to having long played an important and dramatic role in the human cultures of the region (being either an object of veneration or dread), this snake has been a leading cause of snakebite. Each year a multitude of human fatalities are attributed to the Common Cobra, largely because it frequents areas near human dwellings, it possesses a virulent venom, and because locals tend to walk barefoot at night without flashlights.

140

Southern Coral Cobra

Aspidelaps lubricus lubricus

Stocky, two feet long, and pugnacious, this South African snake resembles a miniature cobra. If disturbed as it forages in the evening for lizards, the Southern Coral Cobra will rear up, spread a small hood, and hiss boldly. Favoring semi-arid scrubland and the borders of deserts, this reptile possesses a highly toxic venom, although it is seldom implicated in human envenomings. In the photo at right is a juvenile Southern Coral Cobra.

Rinkhals *Hemachatus haemachatus*

Like many cobra species, the Rinkhals can defend itself by squirting its venom with considerable accuracy, striking its antagonist in the eyes. This is accomplished because the opening in each fang is directed forward. If this technique fails, the Rinkhals is also adept at feigning death, much like the North American Hognose Snakes. Averaging about three feet in length, this species occupies a variety of habitats from sea-level up to over 8,000 feet above sea-level. It is a native of South Africa, where it occurs in the eastern regions. There is a single record from neighboring Mozambique. The young are born alive, and the diet includes most small vertebrates, although toads are preferred.

Western Shield-nosed Cobra

Aspidelaps scutatus scutatus

Robust burrowers, the Shield-nosed Snakes are cobra-like elapids that live in southern Africa from Namibia, Botswana, and Zimbabwe to Transvaal and South Africa to Mozambique. These 15-inch savanna dwellers root about, using their wedge-shaped snouts to maneuver in rodent burrows. Nocturnal, this species hunts for amphibians, lizards, and small mammals. The Shield-nosed Snake is an egg layer. Its venom has caused human fatality although bites are rare.

BK

Collett's Snake *Pseudechis colletti*

Reaching lengths in excess of eight feet, this venomous reptile is native to a small region in northeastern Australia. It uses deep cracks in the soil and fallen timber for shelter. It is nocturnal and crepuscular (active at dawn and dusk) and is an egg-layer.

Eastern Green Mamba *Dendroaspis angusticeps* (below)

This beautiful treesnake is primarily from the forested lowlands of southeast Africa. It is big, averaging five to six feet in length, slender, and brilliant green, like the leaves through which it glides. Swift and graceful like all mambas, this snake hunts by day for birds, rodents, and bats. It ranges from coastal woodlands in Kenya (where it can be abundant) through Tanzania and Mozambique to Natal and northern South Africa, Zimbabwe, and Malawi.

BK

143

California Striped Racer *Masticophis lateralis lateralis*

This conspicuous, five-foot snake prowls rocky slopes, scrublands, and grassy meadows by day in search of lizards and other small vertebrates. Its range includes California in the US and adjacent Baja California in Mexico.

Eastern Rufous-beaked Snake

Rhamphiophis oxyrhynchus rostratus

A resident of sandy thorn or bushveld country in eastern Africa, this three-to-five-foot snake ranges from southern Sudan, Ethiopia, and Somalia south through Kenya, Tanzania, Malawi and Mozambique to Zimbabwe and the eastern Transvaal. Living chiefly in gerbil burrows, this reptile hunts for insects, reptiles, amphibians, and small mammals which it subdues with its mild venom. This species is harmless to humans. Females deposit from eight to seventeen eggs over a period of several days.

Common Boomslang *Dispholidus typus typus*

This slender, five-to-six-foot arboreal snake lives in African savannas, from Senegal and Ethiopia in the north to the Cape Peninsula in the south. One of Africa's most common and widely distributed snakes, the Boomslang can be found in shrubs and trees in open bush country, scrub land, and dry woods. It spends the majority of its time off the ground where it waits motionless in ambush for the chameleons and other lizard which form the principal part of its diet. Highly variable, specimens may be gray, green, yellow or a host of other colors, a fact which has given rise to its many local names in Africa. Females deposit about a dozen eggs during the warm season. This is one of the few snake species bearing fangs at the rear of the mouth that possesses a venom sufficiently virulent to kill a human. However, because of the inoffensive nature of the Boomslang, fewer than twenty deaths have been recorded during the past half-century.

Namib Sand Snake

*Psammophis
leightoni namibiensis*

Alert and fast-moving, sand snakes dart about savannas and deserts chasing small rodents and lizards, or occasionally, other snakes. Sometimes reaching four feet in length, the Namib Sand Snake occurs in Namaqualand, across the Namib Desert, and into southern Angola, Africa.

Common Egg-eater swallowing a bird's egg in the nest.

Brown Egg-eater (*Daspyeltis inornata*) with a chicken egg.

Common Egg-eater *Dasypeltis scabra*

This slender, three-foot snake is found in eastern and southern Africa, from Gambia east to Sudan, Ethiopia, Somalia, and southern Arabia, south to the tip of the continent. These remarkable snakes have special projections from the vertebrae into the gullet which they use to perforate the bird eggs upon which they subsist. They are capable of phenomenal feats of stretching as they swallow their food. When threatened, these harmless egg-layers attempt to bluff their attacker with a show of false bravado followed by an ominous rasping sound they create by rubbing their scales together. Because they resemble several of the local venomous snake species, egg-eaters are often slain by local residents.

South American Cribo *Drymarchon corais corais*

This is one of, if not the longest, colubrid snake in the Western Hemisphere. It ranges through forest edge, savanna, and marshy regions throughout northern South America. It feeds on a variety of vertebrates, but favors toads, frogs, and reptiles. The Cribo is part of a complex that extends through Central America into the southern part of the United States. The representative in Florida, known as the Eastern Indigo Snake, is familiar to many. Cribos are egg-layers, and they tend to be active during the daylight hours.

Cape File Snake *Mehelya capensis capensis*

This powerful, four-foot reptile is a resident of sub-equatorial Africa, ranging from Namibia east to Tanzania and south to Natal. A formidable predator on other snakes, the Cape File Snake also feeds on lizards, amphibians and occasionally small mammals. It is given a wide berth by locals because of its venomous appearance, but this harmless egg-layer is sluggish and inoffensive.

Mussurana (hatchling)
Clelia clelia clelia

Although they are born in bright red garb, Mussuranas lose this color as they age, and adults are uniformly shiny black. Both a powerful constrictor and possessed of venom-conducting fangs at the rear of the mouth, this snake is an efficient predator, capturing and consuming snakes of all kinds. Even large pitvipers are no match for its strength. In spite of this, the Mussurana is a gentle species, seldom attempting to bite humans. This reptile is distributed from Mexico south through much of northern South America and the Amazon Basin. A large snake, the Mussurana commonly exceeds seven feet in length.

Amazon Scarlet Snake
Pseudoboa coronata

Like its relative the Mussurana, the Amazon Scarlet Snake is a predator on reptiles. Usually three feet or less in length, this brilliantly colored snake hunts at night in rainforests of the Amazon Basin of South America. Possibly protected from predators who might find the red color startling, the Scarlet Snake also is adept at fleeing its enemies.

Green Vinesnake
Oxybelis fulgidus

Superbly designed for life in the trees, this swift, alert snake, with its pointed head and leafy coloration, is difficult to detect within the vegetation. The Green Vinesnake ranges widely from Mexico south to Bolivia, usually inhabiting rainforest or gallery forest. Adept at capturing birds, this species will sometimes position itself beside a flower and wait for a hummingbird to approach. Vinesnakes are egg-layers, and they may reach lengths in excess of six feet.

Buff-striped Keelback *Amphiesma stolata*

A common and familiar snake, the Buff-Striped Keelback is distributed from Pakistan and Sri Lanka through southern Asia and Indochina into southern China, Taiwan, and many outlying islands. It is a snake of the lowlands, and especially favors moist areas where the frogs, toads, fishes and earthworms that constitute its diet can be found. This reptile reaches a length of over 30 inches, but averages about 20 inches.

Balsas Groundsnake

Sonora michoacanensis michoacanensis

Groundsnakes are small, seldom exceeding 12 inches, and they spend most of their lives hidden away beneath logs, stones or debris. Yet some varieties, such as the Balsas Groundsnake, exhibit startling colors and patterns. Found in western Mexico, this gaudy reptile feeds on small invertebrates and lays its eggs among humus or similar material.

Andean Whipsnake

Chironius monticola

The Andes of Venezuela south to Bolivia, at intermediate elevations, are criss-crossed with streams and moist forests. This is home to the world's greatest amphibian diversity, and where there are frogs, there are creatures that consume frogs. The Andean Whipsnake, five feet of shimmering green, cruises alertly through the streamside vegetation by day, in quest of frogs. At night, this reptile coils high in the brush to sleep. Its eggs are deposited in decaying vegetation.

WL

Common Liana Snake *Siphlophis cervinus*

This rainforest snake ranges from Panama and Trinidad south to Bolivia. Apparently seldom seen by humans, the Liana Snake is strictly nocturnal, spending much of its time in trees and shrubs in rainforest. Lizards are its preferred prey, and this snake reproduces via eggs.

PC

Northern Speckled Racer

Drymobius margaritiferus margaritiferus

Fast and slender, this attractive three-foot reptile is a locally common inhabitant of stream banks and wet lowland forest from extreme southern Texas in the US, south along the Caribbean versant (one side of a sloping landform) of Mexico and Central America to northern Colombia in South America. Its diet consists almost entirely of frogs.

South American Bushmaster *Lachesis muta*

The Bushmaster reaches a length of at least ten feet and reports abound of much larger animals. This sluggish pitviper lives in primary rainforest and foothill forest east of the Andes in the Amazon Basin and in Brazil's Atlantic Forest. Mammal burrows and large, fallen trees are favored retreats, but this snake also coils motionless on the forest floor for days at a time, waiting for a spiny rat or some other mammal to pass within reach.

Introduction to Seasnakes

Seasnakes can remain submerged for up to one hour and can dive to 165 feet or more. Most seasnakes feed on fish, although two species eat the eggs of fish. Seasnake babies are born live in the water, although Sea Kraits go ashore to lay eggs. Seasnake venom is among the most potent in the animal world. But, seasnakes are not aggressive and human bites are usually the result of the snake being trapped in a fisherman's net. Such bites, however, may be fatal.

Pelagic Seasnake *Pelamis platurus*

Also called the Yellow-Bellied Seasnake, this snake has the widest range of any snake in the world. It occurs in warm seas of the tropical zone from eastern Africa through the Indo-Australian Archipelago, and across the Pacific to the Western Hemisphere. In the New World it has been found as far north as San Clemente, California (US) and as far south as Islas de Pascua in Chile. Seldom over 30 inches in length, this snake lives in the open sea and is most often seen in shallow, offshore waters where it hunts for minnows among flotsam. Like all seasnakes, this species possesses a virulent venom, but it is generally inoffensive. It can swim both forwards and backwards with the help of its flattened tail.

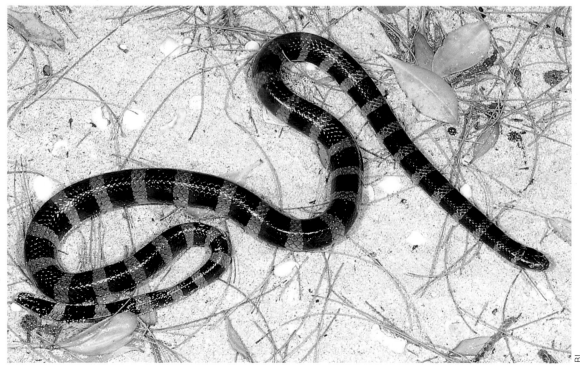

Large-scaled Sea Krait
Laticauda laticaudata

This beautiful, 40-inch seasnake is found in shallow tropical seas from the Bay of Bengal east to Japan's Ryukyu Islands and south to New Guinea, the Coral Sea and west to Fiji. Sea Kraits spend considerable time on land, taking refuge along rocky shores or in mangrove swamps, often far from the sea. Although they possess a toxic venom, Sea Kraits are inoffensive animals, reluctant to bite even when provoked. Females lay up to 14 eggs on land. All other seasnakes are live bearers.

*F*ascinating creatures, amphibians in one form or another have occupied the earth for over 350 million years. They are vertebrates possessing certain skull and backbone modifications that separate them from other groups of organisms. Although many amphibians spend all or most of their lives in the water, there are others that do not, and some are entirely terrestrial. All are ectotherms, deriving most of their body temperature from their surroundings. Their unusual lifestyles, humorous bug-eyed countenances, brilliant colors, and dramatic voices have combined to make these creatures the object of increasing interest world-wide.

There are three major lineages of living amphibians: caecilians, salamanders (includes newts), and frogs (includes toads). They comprise over 4500 species, and many more are yet to be discovered and named. In spite of shared traits, there is some question whether these lineages evolved from a common ancestor or have separate origins. What does seem certain is that the first amphibians arose from a group of bony fishes (Class Osteichthys) that had occupied both marine and freshwater environments at the time amphibians first appeared.

Modern amphibians scarcely resemble their large, armored ancestors. Most are small creatures, although one kind of salamander reaches a length of five feet, and there is a caecilian of similar length. The largest frog, *Conraua goliath*, is only about 14 inches long. As a group, amphibians possess many novel characteristics. These include specialized, replaceable teeth, unique visual cells in their eyes, auditory systems capable of detecting low-frequency sounds, ribs that do not encircle the body, and eyes that can be lowered or raised. They have two kinds of skin glands which secrete mucous for moisture and poisons for defense.

Amphibians are intermediate between terrestrial organisms and fishes in terms of internal anatomy. They possess three-chambered hearts and paired lungs, although the lungs are absent or evolved to a reduced size in some groups. They do not have claws, nails, or hooves, which are a hallmark of terrestrial vertebrates. The skin is glandular, usually moist, and lacks external scales or other adornments.

Both internal and external modes of reproduction are found among the amphibians. Some lay terrestrial eggs which undergo direct development. Some produce aquatic eggs that hatch into larvae. Still others produce live young. Depending on the kind of amphibian, eggs may be laid in burrows, in foam nests on the ground, or high in trees stuck in gelatinous masses on leaves. Some amphibians carry eggs in their mouths, others on their backs, or some even in their stomachs. The eggs are vulnerable to drying, even those deposited on land, as they lack a true shell, and are protected instead by mucous capsules. Those amphibians with an aquatic larval stage undergo extreme changes; perhaps the best known example is from tadpole to frog. The change from larva to adult is called metamorphosis, a process which is not exclusive to amphibians or even vertebrates. Metamorphosis is a complex form of development under the control of the endocrine system, which sends chemical commands through the circulatory system. Breeding styles range from single pairs of animals to loud choruses of frogs, often numbering hundreds of individuals. Frog vocalizations are unique to each species and critical to mate attraction.

Amphibian diets and feeding strategies are a function of size, abundance and seasonality of prey. There are other factors including ecological constraints. Many amphibians are indiscriminate and opportunistic predators, but others are highly specialized. Diets may shift as the species in question matures. Larval amphibians of many species are herbivorous. One frog and some salamander species may be at least partially herbivorous as adults. Insects, and other invertebrates make up the diets of most amphibians, but some species, especially frogs, can be voracious predators. They have been known to feed on reptiles, other amphibians, birds, mammals, mollusks, and even marine invertebrates.

The forty-one families of amphibians collectively exploit a variety of habitats around the world, although most are found in humid tropical regions. In spite of their dependence on moisture, some amphibians spend most of their lives buried while they wait for infrequent desert rains. Some limbless caecilians live in piles of humus or loose soil, while others spend their lives in rivers or lakes. Salamanders can be found in and under logs, beneath stones, in crevices, on leaves, in ponds and lakes, and even in Arctic conditions. Frogs live in swamps, lakes, and rivers, in temperate and tropical forests, and in savannas and deserts. Amphibians are found all over the world, with the exception of Antarctica and some oceanic islands.

Not surprisingly, amphibians have played important roles in folklore and other aspects of human culture. They have been the object of commerce: as food items, pets, medical ingredients, and as animals for research and teaching. In the U. S., an annual frog jumping contest has made national news for at least a century.

Recently, amphibians have become the object of international concern because of their decline or disappearance in some regions in which they were formerly abundant. This alarming development continues to be investigated and appears to be the result of diverse factors (some natural), including increased ultraviolet radiation because of the depleted ozone layer in our atmosphere, a situation that can be lethal to aquatic eggs. Another cause of decline is the exploitation of tropical rainforests as a result of the human population explosion. Scientists have learned that amphibians are finely tuned to the habitats where they live, and as such provide a means by which we can measure environmental degradation.

SALAMANDERS AND NEWTS

Although salamanders and newts, the tailed amphibians, are often thought to be distinct from one another, in actuality newts are simply salamanders that are aquatic as adults. The name "salamander" derives from Greek and Latin, and means "fire lizard." This refers to supposed heat resistance demonstrated when these delicate creatures were seen fleeing logs that had been tossed onto a fire. Salamanders are typically slender. They have tails and one, or more commonly, two pairs of limbs. They lack the distinctive voice possessed by most frogs.

There are ten families and nearly 400 species of salamanders. Most are from temperate regions. The greatest diversity exists in North America, followed by Eurasia. One family extends through Central America into northern South America. Most species are but a few inches in length, although one can reach five feet.

Salamanders of one kind or another can be found in aquatic, subterranean, or arboreal habitats. Their skins have a permeable nature, and moisture is essential to survival, thus they are not found in harsh, dry environments. Some are cave occupants and possess only vestigial eyes. Still others have wedge-shaped heads specialized for burrowing.

Aside from humans, predators of salamanders include reptiles, amphibians, birds, mammals, fishes, and some invertebrates. Collectively, salamanders possess an arsenal of evasive tactics, including tail lashing, toxic skin secretions (some of which can be squirted), and protrusible spines which make them hard for predators to swallow. Salamanders prey on small invertebrates, although some larger aquatic varieties feed on both plant and animal matter.

Distinguished by unique skeletal structures, there are three principal lineages within the salamanders: the Sirens, the Primitive (Giant and Asiatic) Salamanders, and the Advanced Salamanders. The Advanced Salamanders include Newts, Brook, Lungless, and Fire Salamanders, Amphiumas, Waterdogs, Mudpuppies, the Olm, Mole, and Pacific Mole Salamanders.

Sirens are eel-like, aquatic, have external gills, and are restricted to southeastern North America.

Fertilization is external, and eggs are laid in swamps and ponds. Sirens range in size from several inches to over three feet in length.

The Primitive Salamanders consist of two distantly related families: the Giant Salamanders, including the North American Hellbenders, which are the world's largest amphibians; and the much smaller Asiatic Salamanders found in northeastern Asia. Giant Salamanders range in size from the thirty-inch Hellbenders to the five-foot Japanese Giant Salamander. Fertilization is external and free-living larvae hatch from the aquatic eggs. The Advanced Salamanders include six living families and at least 350 species. They are distributed broadly across North America and Eurasia. All have internal fertilization, and some retain larval characteristics throughout life.

Advanced Salamanders include families strongly diverging in habits and appearance. Amphiumas are entirely aquatic, eel-like, and possess greatly reduced limbs. Other Advanced Salamanders are robust, and either aquatic with external gills (Waterdogs) or terrestrial, returning to the water to breed (Mole Salamanders). Newts and their relatives are found mostly in Europe and parts of Asia, although some species occur in North America. These Advanced Salamanders possess toxic skin secretions and are often brightly colored as a warning to predators. Some species undergo a lengthy terrestrial stage as juveniles before they return to water as adults.

By far the most species-rich group of Advanced Salamanders (indeed, of all salamanders) are the lungless salamanders of the family Plethodontidae. This group includes 257 species that primarily occupy upland mountain forests, but some are also found in tropical America. This group is entirely confined to the Western Hemisphere except for three species of the genus *Hydromantoides* occurring in France and Italy. Respiration is through the skin, and many lungless salamander species lead entirely terrestrial lives, without larval stages or aquatic eggs. Some members of the Plethodontid genus *Oedipina* are bizarrely slender, with reduced limbs, while other genera include more robust species.

Fire Salamander *Salamandra salamandra ssp.*

The Fire Salamander has been known for centuries to residents of south and central Europe, and even figures in mythological accounts from the region. Its common name derives from the sudden, "magical" appearance of these amphibians from logs thrown onto a winter fire. In truth, the hibernating salamanders simply are fleeing the flames. Their brilliant coloration serves as a warning to predators, as their skin contains toxic secretions. Usually inactive by day, this species is terrestrial except when females enter the water to deposit their larvae, which are born alive. This eight-inch, stocky, insect-eater has been found as high as 6500 feet above sea-level.

Above, the Striped Fire Salamander, *Salamandra salamandra terrestris*

Eastern Tiger Salamander
Ambystoma tigrinum

Like other members of the Mole Salamander family, these 13-inch amphibians spend much of their lives underground in rodent burrows and similar situations. Winter and early spring rains cause them to emerge and enter ponds to breed. Aquatic larvae hatch from eggs and later emerge as terrestrial adults. Many color variations are found throughout the eastern half of the US, but usually Eastern Tiger Salamanders are yellow and gray-to-black. They feed voraciously on insects and tiny vertebrates. They also eat many earthworms.

Marbled Salamander *Ambystoma opacum*

This plump, banded salamander lives beneath logs in wooded and semi-open areas over much of the eastern US. It is able to tolerate somewhat drier conditions than many amphibians, and it actually lays its eggs on the ground rather than in water. After laying her eggs in the autumn, the female guards them until heavy rains stimulate hatching. The diet of this five-inch salamander consists of small invertebrates.

Red Salamander *Pseudotriton ruber sp.*

This salamander makes its home in or near clear, cool, upland waters in the eastern U.S. It lives beneath logs, moss, or stones and can be found in open fields as well as woodland. Large adults can measure up to six inches in length. They feed on small invertebrates.

Northern Long-toed Salamander

Ambystoma macrodactylum krausei

This three-inch amphibian spends its life beneath debris along streams and lakes in the northwestern US and Canada. It can tolerate cold temperatures and has even been found entering the water to breed when ice was present. An occupant of alpine and subalpine zones, this species is found from 3,500 feet to over 6,000 feet above sea-level. It feeds on small arthropods.

Spotted Salamander
Ambystoma maculatum

At nine inches in length, the Spotted Salamander is one of the largest and most handsome amphibians in North America. After spending nearly the entire year hidden beneath the ground in moist woodlands, warm spring rains cause them to emerge in droves and enter shallow pools to mate and lay eggs. Upon completion of breeding, adults return to a life underground. The aquatic larvae feed on small invertebrates, while adults make a diet of earthworms and insects. Spotted Salamanders are found from central and eastern Canada south to Georgia and east Texas.

Monterey Ensatina
Ensatina eschscholtzii eschscholtzii

Native to both clearings and wooded areas of south-central California, the Monterey Ensatina spends most of its life hiding in rotten logs or concealed in rodent burrows. When threatened, Ensatinas typically arch the tail, sway the back, and lock their legs in an upright position. Females brood the eggs underground. This salamander preys on insects.

Japanese Fire-bellied Newt
Cynops pyrrhogaster

This newt is hardy in captivity and has for many years been a staple of the aquarium trade. In its native Honshu, Shikoku and Kyoto, Japan, it occupies standing waters which are usually thickly vegetated.

Mandarin Crocodile Newt
Tylototriton shanjing

This eight-inch sala-mander is found in the mountains of western Yunnan Province, China, and probably in neighboring Myanmar (Burma). It was recognized as a species in 1995. Perhaps its startling color pattern and shape gave it the name, "shanjing," which translates as "mountain demon."

Stephen Dalton/NHPA

Axolotl

Ambystoma mexicanum

Known today from a single lake, Xochimilco, in central Mexico, this near-mythical creature breeds readily under laboratory conditions. Because of this, it has long figured in experimental biology. Axolotls retain their larval characteristics into adulthood, unlike most salmanders. While metamorphosed adults have been found, this salamander breeds and functions as an adult while continuing the use of gills and the aquatic lifestyle of the larvae. Axolotls, perhaps because of their strange appearance, figure prominently in pre-Columbian legends. In more recent times they have served as a food source to regional inhabitants. The prey consists of small invertebrates.

DB

*C*aecilians in general are rather drab, worm-like amphibians, with some exceptions. Two species which are more interesting in appearance have been included in this book. There are six families and 163 species of caecilians recognized today by science. These are limbless, elongate animals. Nearly blind, their eyes are covered by a thin layer of bone or skin. Some caecilians possess dermal scales, but these are not evident externally. Fertilization is internal, with some species retaining eggs in the body cavity and producing aquatic larvae, while others lay eggs that develop directly into terrestrial young. Most caecilians are gray, dark blue, or pink in color, and lack a pattern. They remain among the least-known and most poorly understood of all amphibians. Occupants of the world's humid tropical regions, caecilians are adapted to life either in the water or underground in burrows or humus. Most caecilians measure less than two feet in length, but some can exceed four feet. Aquatic species feed on fishes and small invertebrates while terrestrial forms feed primarily on earthworms.

Usambara Caecilian *Boulengerula boulengeri*

Wormlike in appearance, this nine-inch amphibian lives in loose soil and forest litter in northeastern Tanzania, Africa. It eats earthworms. Caecilians are usually seen at the surface only after heavy showers or during the evening.

Koh Tao Caecilian *Ichthyophis kohtaoensis*

This foot-long amphibian is found in rainforest and other lowland tropical habitats in Thailand and the Malay Peninsula. It makes its home in leaf litter, humus, and loose soil where it hunts for the worms and small insects that comprise its diet.

*E*asily the most conspicuous and best-known of amphibians, frogs comprise 25 families containing 334 genera and over 3900 species. These short-bodied amphibians lack tails. They possess elongate hind-limbs and some unique modifications in the vertebral column which enable them to leap, swim, and burrow. Frogs range in size from less than half an inch to about 14 inches in length. Some species are truly amphibious, spending their lives in and out of the water, while others are entirely aquatic or terrestrial.

World-wide in distribution, frogs can be found on every continent except Antarctica, and in every habitat except the driest deserts and the polar regions. Some species occur within the Arctic Circle. They are present on most oceanic islands. Most frogs are tropical, but they are well-represented in temperate regions.

Fertilization in the great majority of species is external. Eggs are deposited in the water or in a moist place on the ground. Larvae, which are aquatic, undergo an extraordinary metamorphosis as they pass into adulthood. In some varieties, tiny froglets emerge from the egg in what is called direct development.

Most frogs possess smooth, moist skins, while toads tend to be warty and drier-skinned. However, this distinction is not universal, and is reversed in some cases. The difference between the two is basically semantic, as all toads are frogs.

Many frogs are capable of vocalization, and their calls are distinctive. Individuals gather to breed at a swamp, pond, lake or stream. These breeding aggregations can number into the thousands, and their collective calls can be heard over great distances. Mating is usually considered to be stimulated by season, day length, and rainfall. According to the species, eggs may be deposited on leaves overhanging water-filled depressions, in tree-holes, in shallow depressions created by the male, in terrestrial or arboreal foam nests made by females, in burrows, or directly into the water. Some species produce massive quantities of eggs while others may lay only a few.

Parental care is exhibited by some species. Some brood the eggs in the back, stomach, or mouth of an adult. Some sit with the eggs or transport eggs or tadpoles on the back. Frog larvae, or tadpoles, may metamorphose after a few days or several years, according to the species. Most tadpoles are vegetarians, but some species are carnivores or even cannibals.

Frogs are preyed on by many kinds of organisms, including man. Defensive tactics vary but include leaping or swimming away, camouflage, crypsis (resembling one's surroundings), threat displays, distasteful or toxic skin secretions, loud vocalizations, feigning death, and biting. Some toxic species, most notably the Poison Frogs of Latin America, display brilliant warning colors.

Frogs in turn prey on almost anything small enough to be subdued. Most are voracious predators. Insects and other small invertebrates comprise the principal prey items, but larger species feed on reptiles, amphibians, small mammals and birds, and some are cannibals. At least one species, *Hyla truncata*, consumes plants.

There are great diversity and varying degrees of divergence among frog groups. This has caused much disagreement with regard to higher classification. Generally, there are three major lineages: Primitive Frogs, Transitional Frogs, and Advanced Frogs.

Primitive Frogs include the so-called Tailed, New Zealand, and Disk-Tongued Frogs. There are twenty species divided into seven genera. They range from western Asia to New Zealand and northwest North America. The Tailed Frog practices internal fertilization and parental care is exhibited by several other Primitive Frog species. The terrestrial New Zealand Frog is the only native amphibian in that country and possesses rib structures that are unique. Disk-tongued Frogs have vertically elliptical or triangular pupils and possess a number of unique internal modifications.

Transitional Frogs include the Clawed, Suriname, Burrowing, and Spadefoot Toads, Asian Leaf, and Parsley Frogs. One hundred sixteen species are divided into 15 genera found in North America, Central and South America, Eurasia, Southeast Asia, and Africa. Clawed Frogs have played an important role in medical research. The bizarre, flattened Suriname Toad broods its eggs in pockets that form on the back of the adult female. The Burrowing Toad, a strange subterranean creature, lives on termites and ants, emerging only to breed. Spadefoot Toads, Asian Leaf Frogs, and Parsley Frogs have vertical pupils, and Spadefoots possess specialized, hardened structures on the hind feet for digging.

Advanced Frogs comprise all remaining species and these are subdivided into three lineages. One is the Narrow Mouthed Frogs: chunky, terrestrial, burrowing species distributed over parts of eastern Asia, North and Central America. A second includes typical frogs of the genus *Rana*, found world-wide in

both aquatic and terrestrial species; it also includes colorful Reed Frogs of Africa, and the Old World Treefrogs of Africa and Asia. The third group contains a dozen families including typical toads and their relatives. This group also includes the beautiful Poison Frogs from Latin America, the Paradox Frogs, Slender-fingered Frogs, Glass Frogs, and two families of Treefrogs. Granite Frogs from the Seychelles Islands may be part of this or the previous lineage.

Blue Poison Frog *Dendrobates azureus*

161

Red-eyed Leaf Frog
Agalychnis callidryas

Perhaps the most photographed of all amphibians, this remarkable creature has become the very symbol of the rainforest. Its specific name *callidryas* derives from the Greek *kallos*, meaning beautiful, and *dryas*, a tree nymph. It becomes active at twilight after a day spent in slumber among treetop leaves. When it glances about, its huge eyes look like crimson headlights. This three-inch frog moves, marsupial-like, among the branches as it forages for insects.

Arrival of the wet season in the great pluvial (rain drenched) forests from Veracruz, Mexico, to eastern Panama, means breeding time for this species. Males call from branches overhanging woodland pools to attract their mates. Deftly rolling a leaf into a funnel, the female deposits her eggs so that emerging tadpoles will tumble into the water below.

At left, a Red-eyed Leaf Frog sheltering from the rain, and below, a male Red-eyed Leaf Frog attempts to interfere with an amplectant (mating) pair.

Introduction to Treefrogs (Family Hylidae)

Hylid frogs are distributed worldwide and the family as currently recognized includes 43 genera and 719 species. The greatest species diversity is reached in the genus *Hyla* in the Americas, especially in the tropical zones of Central and South America. Many kinds of treefrogs have become familiar to the public, as their images (graceful, attractive, or humorous) have been used for calendars, posters, and advertisements. As their name implies, these amphibians are adapted for a climbing life, usually in trees and shrubs, using their expanded toe pads like miniature suction cups to aid them in perching and leaping adroitly through vegetation, or sometimes on rocks. In the Americas, treefrogs can be found from marshes and steamy lowland forests to cool mountain woodlands and chilly sub-alpine zones, from Canada to southern South America.

Treefrogs have generally high moisture requirements, so they secrete themselves by day into crevices, beneath bark, or among leaves so that they can avoid dehydration. Nighttime, with milder temperatures and higher humidity, is when most treefrogs become active. Ranging from diminutive amphibians of less than one inch to impressive gargantuans the size of an outstretched human hand, nearly all treefrogs exist on a diet of insects. In the majority of cases, eggs are laid in the water or in sticky masses on leaves.

Like all Leaf Frogs (genera *Agalychnis* and *Phyllomedusa*), Red-eyed Leaf Frogs must contend with the problem of how to retain moisture during the day. Sleeping high in the trees, these amphibians are vulnerable to dessication from breezes. Leaf Frogs possess special wax-producing glands in the skin, and they wipe the secretions all over themselves, creating a cuticle that holds moisture inside the frog.

The eggs, deposited in rolled leaves above the water, also are vulnerable to drying. To combat this, females lay eggless capsules, filled with water, among the fertile eggs. These capsules release their moisture slowly so that the clutch will not dessicate.

There is considerable geographic variation among populations of the Red-eyed Leaf Frog, with some areas having large and colorful specimens while other regions produce small and somewhat drab individuals.

PC

Above, a Red-eyed Leaf Frog walking.

Below, a Splendid Leaf Frog, *Agalychnis calcarifer*

GS

The Red-eyed Leaf Frog above has brilliant blue markings. Compare this specimen to the frog at the top of the previous page. Although they are the same species, there is considerable color variation. Such color differences can be seen in isolated populations that may be only a few miles from each other.

Barred Leaf Frog *Phyllomedusa tomopterna* (below)

Found throughout the Amazon Basin of South America, this ornate amphibian lives in trees, sleeping concealed among the leaves by day and clambering slowly about in search of insects by night. Like most Leaf Frogs, its call is barely audible.

PC

Chaco Leaf Frog *Phyllomedusa sauvagii*

This unusual frog, prone to walk slowly rather than jump, is adapted for life in the harsh Chaco of Bolivia, Paraguay, northern Argentina, and adjacent Brazil. Special glands in its skin secrete a waxy substance with which this three-and-one-half-inch amphibian paints itself to prevent water loss while it rests during the day. Females, stimulated by rains, deposit their eggs in sticky masses on leaves above water. The emergent tadpoles fall into the water and complete their life cycle. The Chaco Leaf Frog eats small invertebrates.

GS

WL

Giant Monkey Frog *Phyllomedusa bicolor*

Plodding deliberately through the rainforest vegetation in the Amazon Basin, Monkey Frogs look more like wind-up toys than legitimate creatures. Robust of build and nearly six inches long, an adult ranks as one of the largest of the world's treefrogs. Like the other Leaf Frogs with which it comprises a group, this nocturnal amphibian sleeps beneath a waxy cuticle secreted by special glands in their skin.

Awakening at dusk from its slumber, the Monkey Frog ambles about in the trees, using its enormous owl-like eyes to detect insect prey. Some Indian tribes in the upper Amazon make use of sophisticated alkaloid compounds in the skin of this creature. Small amounts in the bloodstream greatly enhance vision and reputedly aid in the task of hunting.

Savanna Leaf Frog *Phyllomedusa hypocondrialis*

Like other members of its genus, the Savannah Leaf Frog is capable of sealing its skin with a waxy secretion to ward off the dessicating effects of high heat as it sleeps by day. It is a denizen of more open, forested areas from Colombia, Venezuela, and the Guianas. It is replaced to the south in Paraguay, southeastern Brazil, and Argentina, by its close relative *Phyllomedusa azurea.* Prowling slowly through vegetation at night, these deliberate amphibians are reminiscent of chameleons, especially in their ability to grasp. Food consists of small insects. This frog lays its eggs in sticky, gelatinous masses on leaves overhanging quiet pools of water.

Note the unusual grasping ability of leaf frogs.

Warty Leaf Frog *Phyllomedusa tarsius* (right)

At over four inches in length, the Warty Leaf Frog ranks as one of the largest of all Leaf Frogs. Also, it has a very distinctive eye, with gold reticulations on a black background. This frog lives in Amazonian rainforests in South America. It sleeps by day in the trees and hunts for insects at night, only descending to breed around forest pools. Females deposit their eggs in sticky masses that adhere to leaves above the water.

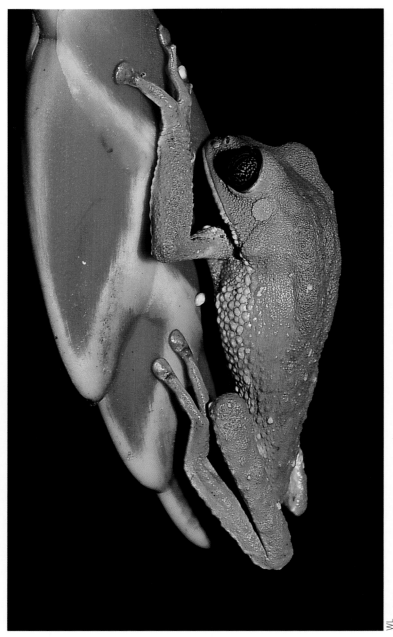

Amazon Leaf Frog *Agalychnis craspedopus* (left and below)

This spectacular amphibian is rarely seen by humans because it spends its life concealed high in the canopy of the rainforest. It descends only to breed over isolated pools in hollow stumps and logs. Females, which are larger than males, can reach a length of nearly five inches. This frog is known only from Colombia, Ecuador and Peru.

White's Treefrog *Pelodryas caerulea*

A native of northwestern Australia (where it is called the Green Treefrog) and southern New Guinea, this four-inch amphibian is found in a wide variety of habitats, including human dwellings. The call, a deep *"wark-wark-wark,"* is heard emanating from flooded grassy areas where these frogs breed. Old adults, with their excess of fatty tissue, take on a comically human appearance, appearing to smile. The diet consists of insects and occasionally small vertebrates.

Common Polkadot Treefrog *Hyla punctata punctata*

Brilliant green with red (and sometimes yellow) polkadots by day, this treefrog becomes almost entirely red at night (the partially red frog in the photo below is in transition between these colors). It is common in marshy areas along river borders, lakes, and flooded grasslands of lowland South America from Trinidad south to the Paraguayan Chaco, east of the Andes mountains. About two inches in length, males call from the water surface in grassy areas. About 200-400 eggs are deposited in the water. The diet consists of small invertebrates.

Casque-headed Treefrog

Hemiphractus proboscideus

This bizarre, Amazonian, forest-dwelling frog is a perfect mimic of the dead, crinkled leaves among which it hides. The fleshy appendages and head shape render it even more difficult to discern as it sits motionless on the forest floor or in low vegetation. Nocturnal and uncommon, Casqueheads feed on small frogs and insects which they subdue with their vise-like jaws. When threatened, they often gape, revealing their yellow tongue.

Pacific Green Treefrog

Hyla pellucens

A frog of lowland humid forest and semi-open areas, the Pacific Green Treefrog is found only in western Colombia and adjacent Ecuador along the Pacific coastal plain. It is a common and familiar species yet, as is the case for so many tropical amphibians and reptiles, almost nothing is known of its life history. Adults measure between two and three inches in length. Breeding males call from vegetation on or around the water. Eggs are deposited in a film at the surface.

Hourglass Treefrog *Hyla ebraccata*

Bedecked in yellow and tan or maroon, the one-inch Hourglass Treefrog ranges from the lowlands of southern Mexico through Central America to northwestern Ecuador. Usually, it bears a distinctive hourglass-shaped marking on its back, but this may be replaced by spots or be completely lacking in some specimens. This frog inhabits primary humid forest, and it emerges to breed during heavy rains. Often, it can be found in cut-over areas adjacent to forest or in areas where most of the forest has been removed. In spite of its size, this small amphibian has a distinctive and easily heard voice. Males call from leaves of emergent herbs or vegetation closely overhanging the water. Masses containing from 24 to 76 eggs are laid in shallow pools. Their diet consists of small invertebrates.

Map Treefrog

Hyla geographica

One of the most widespread and conspicuous frogs of Amazonian and Orinocoan South America, this three-inch amphibian has been the object of much investigation. This is because of the unusual herding behavior exhibited by its tadpoles, which move about en masse. The Map Treefrog is highly variable, and young specimens frequently bear little resemblance to adults. One of a group known as Gladiator Frogs because of mating rituals, the Map Treefrog can be found calling at night from vegetation overhanging the water. It eats insects.

Clown Treefrog *Hyla leucophyllata*

Part of a complex of small frogs known for their gaudy garb and unusual herbal odor, the Clown Treefrog is common in tropical lowlands in the Amazon Basin and the Guianas of South America. Its pattern is quite variable, and one phase (frog at right in photo above) is so distinctive that it was for many years regarded incorrectly as a separate species, *Hyla favosa*.

Mottled Clown Frog

Hyla sarayacuensis

This frog is aptly named for its intricate pattern. The Mottled Clown Frog is found in the Upper Amazon Basin of South America where it favors forested pools in which it breeds. Its ratchet-like call can be heard on warm, rainy evenings as these frogs congregate around marshy pools near forests. Less than two inches in length, these colorful amphibians feed on a variety of small insects.

Canyon Treefrog *Hyla arenicolor*

Unlike most treefrogs, this two-inch species uses rocky niches and streambanks for refuge. Native to the mountains and plateau areas of the western US from Utah and Colorado southward as far as Oaxaca, Mexico, the Canyon Treefrog spends most of its time on the ground. It has been found living as high as 10,000 feet above sea-level. Its call is an explosive, machine-like clicking sound.

Barking Treefrog *Hyla gratiosa*

Named for its raucous and distinctive call, this robust two-and-three-quarters-inch amphibian is both a climber and a burrower. For this reason it can withstand harsh temperatures. Aside from a few isolated colonies, this nocturnal insectivore is found along the southeast coastal plain of the US. Breeding groups assemble around water from March to August.

PC

Ornate Horned Frog *Ceratophrys ornata*

Native to the Pampean region of Argentina, Uruguay, and Brazil, Ornate Horned Frogs must endure a dry season each year. In order to conserve vital moisture during this time, they spend a great deal of time underground, protectively enshrouded in a shell-like cuticle (hardened skin) excreted from glands in the skin. The onset of the rainy season arouses these powerful

Introduction to Horned Frogs

Horned frogs are unique: they have huge, powerful jaws, squatty bodies with short legs, and the habit of dining on other frogs. Native to South America, these unusual amphibians spend much of their time sitting in ambush, looking like their surroundings, while they wait for an unsuspecting frog to stray past. Horned frogs possesses powerful jaws capable of clenching prey in a vice-like grasp.

Chaco Horned Frog *Ceratophrys cranwelli*

The Chaco Horned Frog survives by spending much time buried and cloaked in a protective covering secreted by special glands in the skin. It often sits in silt with only its eyes exposed. Its range spans portions of Argentina, Bolivia, Brazil, and Paraguay, an area of harsh extremes, with torrential rains interrupted by searing dry spells. The specimen shown here is a juvenile albino.

four-inch predators, and they emerge to breed and to feed on insects and small animals. One of their preferred food items is other frogs, which they sometimes attract by placing a hindfoot on top of the head and wriggling the toes. Since they blend closely with their marshy surroundings, the toes look like insect prey, so the Ornate Horned Frog is able to lure other amphibians to their deaths, much like a fisherman using a worm.

GS

174

Amazon Horned Frog

Ceratophrys cornuta

Like its relative the Northern Horned Frog, the Amazon Horned Frog is an ambush predator, sitting concealed in the leaf litter of the Amazonian rainforest while waiting for an unwary frog to pass within reach. This species possesses a distinctive, soft, fleshy horn-like structure above each eye, perhaps increasing its resemblance to the leaves in which it hides. Large adults exceed four inches in length.

175

Tomato Frog *Dyscophus antongilii* (above and below)

Plump and red, the adult males of this ubiquitous Madagascan native look very much like their namesake. After passing much of the year in hiding, these amphibians come forth en masse at the onset of spring rains. The smaller, yellow-brown females (below and right) enter temporary pools and produce gelatinous masses containing thousands of eggs. Upon hatching, the tadpoles must mature rapidly or risk death by dehydration when the pools dry up. Tomato Frogs protect themselves through toxic skin secretions. Their diet consists of insects.

Madagascan Burrowing Frog *Dyscophus insularis* (above)

This species is similar to, but about one-half the size of, the closely-related Tomato Frog. It is found in the forests of southern and western Madagascar where it spends its life among the leaf litter or underground.

Northern Glass Frog *Hyalinobatrachium fleischmanni*

Translucent skins have made living anatomy lessons of these tiny, arboreal amphibians. Glass frogs occur in lowland and cloudforest from Mexico south to Bolivia, primarily along rocky mountain and foothill streams. Their breeding call is a plaintive peep. Eggs, laid in a gelatinous mass on a leaf over the water are guarded by the male frog. When they hatch, the tadpoles fall, tumbling through the air, into the stream below.

Meta Glass Frog

Centrolene sp. (new species) (below)

There are three genera and about 96 recognized species of the tiny-to-medium-sized glass frogs. They are distributed from southern Mexico south into northern and central South America. There are many species, including the one illustrated, which have yet to be formally described in a scientific journal. Most glass frogs live along mountain streams where they issue their plaintive peeping calls from high in the trees. Eggs are deposited in a sticky mass on a leaf and then guarded by the male frog.

White-spotted Glass Frog (above)

Cochranella albomaculata

This one-inch frog shares its habitat, rain forests of Costa Rica, Panama, and western Colombia, with several other species of glass frogs. Emerging at dusk from its hiding place, this species spends the night hunting insects among the trees along forest streams. Females encounter calling males on leaves above the water, deposit eggs there, and leave the job of guarding them to the males. Tadpoles emerge and fall into the creek to complete their life cycle. Their diet consists of small insects.

Introduction to Reed Frogs

Hyperolius sp

There are about 112 species in the genus *Hyperolius*; all are small (about one inch in length), most are colorful and complexly patterned, and they are widely distributed throughout sub-Saharan Africa. So variable are Reed Frogs in color and pattern that their relationships are still the subject of ongoing studies. Scientists really aren't sure just how many species exist. As their name implies, these diminutive amphibians spend much of their time in reeds and other vegetation surrounding bodies of water. They emerge to hunt for insects and emit their shrill whistling calls at night.

Painted Reed Frog

Hyperolius marmoratus taeniatus

Abundant throughout its range from Tanzania in East Africa south into the Republic of South Africa, this one-inch frog breeds in nearly any permanent body of water along the coastal plain. Choruses of hundreds of these frogs, calling with a series of piercing whistles, can be heard during warm months. Its diet consists of small insects. This frog is extremely variable in coloration and pattern, and there are many named races.

The Boror Reed Frog above is *Hyperolius argus*. The subspecies of Painted Reed Frog at top right is *Hyperolius marmoratus aposematicus*. Another subspecies just below it is *Hyperolius marmoratus parallelus*.

Pacific Chorus Frog *Hyla (Pseudacris) regilla* (right and below)

This adaptable little frog can be found everywhere from moist, wooded uplands to desert oases, all the way from southwestern Canada through the western US, to Baja California in Mexico. A variety of habitats is acceptable, including chaparral, grasslands, forest, and even agricultural areas. In many parts of its range, it is the most commonly heard frog during warm months. Predominantly a ground dweller, the Pacific Chorus Frog hides by day among vegetation, emerging to feed on small insects at night.

Ornate Chorus Frog *Pseudacris ornata* (left)

Unlike most frogs, this tiny denizen of the southeast US calls only during the cooler winter months; it is more often heard than seen. Its call, a series of high-pitched peeps, is recognized by many persons, who usually don't know the source. Ornate Chorus Frogs live in forest ponds and flooded meadows.

Darwin's Frog *Rhinoderma darwini*

When it comes to bizarre forms of parental care, Darwin's Frog has few peers. A native of temperate forests in southern Chile, this frog lays its eggs on land. When the larvae are ready to emerge, their movements attract any adult males in the area. The males each take one to several eggs into their mouths, pushing them into their vocal pouch with their tongue. The larvae remain there until they have metamorphosed into froglets (tiny frogs), at which time they emerge. Darwin's Frog also has developed a unique method of avoiding predators. It floats, upside down in streams, it's snorkle-like nose and coloration making it resemble a fallen leaf while it drifts to safety.

Green and Golden Bell-frog *Litoria aurea*

A pond-dwelling species from southeastern Australia, this three-inch frog is a voracious predator. It consumes insects and other frogs, including smaller individuals of its own kind. Primarily nocturnal, it seldom strays from the bullrushes in which it typically shelters. During the breeding season, the deep, droning call of the males is commonly heard. Eggs are deposited in floating vegetation.

Giant Treefrog

Litoria infrafrenata (photo at right)

Reaching a length of five and one-half inches, this is one of the world's largest treefrogs. It is a native of humid lowland forests in the Indo-Australian Archipelago.

Coquí *Eleutherodactylus coqui*

Native to Puerto Rico, the Coquí has been accidentally and/or intentionally introduced on St. Croix and St. Thomas, U.S. Virgin Islands, in southern Florida, and Louisiana. Common in its native territory, it occupies moist broadleaf forests up to 3900 feet above sea-level. Members of the genus *Eleutherodactylus*, commonly called "Rain Frogs," number in the hundreds, and are distributed throughout the Caribbean, Central, and South America. Eggs are laid on land and are guarded by the male frog in the nest, which is usually in a rolled leaf or frond. This two-inch frog feeds on a variety of insects and is named for the distinctive sound of its two-note call, *co-quí*.

Little Grass Frog *Pseudacris ocularis*

This frog is the smallest amphibian in the United States. It lives among low vegetation in cypress pools and moist areas along the coast from Virginia through Florida to southeast Alabama. At about one-half inch, this creature is so small it is often mistaken for a juvenile of some other frog species. Its high, tinkling call is barely audible to humans. Its diet includes tiny insects.

Hispaniolan Treefrog *Hyla heilprini* (right)

This two-inch treefrog is native to Hispaniola (Haiti and the Dominican Republic), where it occurs anywhere from sea-level to over 6,000 feet. It favors rapidly flowing streams in wet forest situations. Males emit their ratchet-like call from hiding places, usually in crevices of rocks adjacent to splash zones of waterfalls and similar situations. Once widespread in Haiti, this species has been reduced there because of habitat destruction. Its diet include insects and other small invertebrates.

Dwarf Clown Treefrog

Hyla bifurca

Like its relatives in the Clown Treefrog complex, this one-inch amphibian bears attractive colors and sports a distinctive, herbal odor. Dwarf Clown Treefrogs favor marshy pools and other wet areas adjacent to rainforests in South America's Amazon Basin. Their distinctive call may be heard on warm, rainy nights when choruses assemble. Their diet consists of small insects.

GS

Poison Frogs (Family Dendrobatidae)

Bearing toxic alkaloid compounds in their brilliantly colored skins, these jewels of the rainforest can be found in Central and South America in humid habitats. Their startling colors serve to warn potential predators, such as birds, that danger is at hand. This family of frogs includes nine genera and some 160 species.

Poison Frogs have become internationally known because of the colors and poisons of some of the species. It was long assumed that indigenous people used these toxic creatures to coat their arrows and darts for hunting purposes. In truth, only two species have ever been used in such a manner. Indigenous peoples along the west coast of South America used toxic extracts of the skin of these two species to tip their blowgun darts for hunting, and this has unjustly garnered a reputation for many of the remaining and largely inoffensive species in this family.

However, some Poison Frogs do possess extremely toxic chemicals in their skins. In recent years, dendrobatids have gained popularity as terrarium animals, and many species are bred in captivity today. Their complex skin alkaloids, of considerable importance in pharmacological research, are curiously reduced in captive-born specimens. Perhaps they derive their toxicity from certain insects they consume. Many species use water-filled bromeliads or other temporary pools to release their tadpoles, which the adults transport on their backs.

Phantasmal Poison Frog *Epipedobates tricolor*

PC

Phantasmal Poison Frog *Epipedobates tricolor*

Phantasmal Poison Frog *Epipedobates tricolor*

Phantasmal Poison Frog *Epipedobates tricolor*

Lehmann's Poison Frog *Dendrobates lehmanni*

183

Red-backed Poison Frog *Dendrobates reticulatus*

Granular Poison Frog *Dendrobates granuliferus*

Strawberry Poison Frog *Dendrobates pumilio* (all photos this page)

(Above) The male Strawberry Poison Frog transports its tadpoles from leaves and bromeliad cups to streams and pools and releases them.

Strawberry Poison Frog

Dendrobates pumilio
The two frogs at left show the variety of color of this species.

185

Amazonian Poison Frog *Dendrobates ventrimaculatus*

Green-and-Black Poison Frog *Dendrobates auratus*

Yellow-banded Poison Frog *Dendrobates leucomelas*

Dendrobates (new species, not yet described)

Striped Poison Frog *Phyllobates vittatus* (below)

Mimic Poison Frog *Dendrobates imitator* (below)

Strawberry Poison Frog *Dendrobates pumilio* (left)

187

Harlequin Poison Frog *Dendrobates histrionicus*

Harlequin Poison Frog *Dendrobates histrionicus*

Harlequin Poison Frog *Dendrobates histrionicus*

Dyeing Poison Frog *Dendrobates tinctorius*

Dyeing Poison Frog *Dendrobates tinctorius* (above and left)

Blue Poison Frog *Dendrobates azureus*   **Harlequin Poison Frog** *Dendrobates histrionicus* (below)

Red-legged Running Frog *Kassina maculata*

Nocturnal denizens of swamps and pools, these three-inch amphibians are found from the coastal plain of Kenya south into northeastern Republic of South Africa. Primarily ground dwellers, these frogs congregate around pools of water to breed. Their calls, explosive *quoicks*, are repeated at lengthy intervals at night during the rainy season. The bulging eyes and vertical pupils give adult running frogs a unique appearance.

Island Eyelash Frog *Ceratobatrachus guentheri*

Blending with the tan or yellow leaves of the rainforest floor, this placid four-inch amphibian is able to conceal itself effectively from both enemies and prey. Native to the Solomons and Bougainville Island, these "sit-and-wait" predators bear remarkable resemblance to the Casque-Headed Frogs of the American tropics. Many tropical frogs and toads have patterns, colors, and appendages modified to enhance their resemblance to the leaf litter in which they spend their lives.

Green Cascade Frog *Rana livida*

Members of the cosmopolitan genus *Rana* are referred to as "typical frogs," and the reference befits them: they tend to be long-legged, green, and adept at jumping into the water when threatened. Although many *Rana* do not live in water, their habitat always involves its proximity. Native to southern China, India, Myanmar (Burma), and Vietnam, the Green Cascade Frog lives in streams within forested regions up to about 2000 feet above sea-level. It can still be found on Che Kei Shan, a peak on Hong Kong Island where construction has yet to commence. Much of its time is spent clinging to rocks or hiding in crevices. The skin secretions of this frog are toxic and caustic. Like other members of its genus, this amphibian feeds on insects and lays its eggs in the water.

PC

Red Rain Frog *Scaphiophryne gottlebei*

This odd little frog is known from a single valley in Madagascar. It is terrestrial, favoring rocky locales, where it breeds in shallow pools, often of rainwater. When disturbed, this one-and-one-half-inch amphibian inflates its body with air. Little is known about the habits of this frog. Presumably, it feeds upon small invertebrates.

Spiny-headed Treefrog
Anotheca spinosa

Known from isolated populations in upland tropical forests from southern Mexico to Costa Rica and Panama, this bizarre, four-inch frog is not common anywhere. Perhaps this is because it is adapted to life high in the treetops, where it makes use of water-filled bromeliads and tree hollows for shelter and a place to lay its eggs. Interestingly, the tadpoles feed on eggs laid by the female during part of their development. The call of this frog is loud, presumably because it emanates from a tree hollow.

PMF

Madagascan Marbled Frog (above)
Scaphiophryne marmorata

Found only on Madagascar, Marbled Frogs spend much of the year underground in forested regions up to 4000 feet above sea-level. Aroused by torrential rains, these plump two-inch amphibians emerge en masse to breed in shallow pools. Special modifications on the toes of this species indicate that it may also be capable of climbing. When threatened, adults can inflate the body, as seen in the photo above. The call, eggs, and tadpoles of this species have yet to be described by scientists.

Southern Leopard Frog *Rana sphenocephala* (above and left)

The most common "pond frog" throughout the southeastern US, its presence is usually heralded by a splashing noise as it hurls itself into the water. Long-legged and agile, these four-inch amphibians are adept at jumping and swimming. Most *Rana* are associated with fresh and even brackish water, yet some adults may wander considerable distances over land on humid summer nights during nocturnal forays for food. Males produce their short, barking trill from concealed positions in the water, and this species is known to be a prolific breeder. Eggs are laid in gelatinous masses just below the water's surface, and the emergent tadpoles play an important role as food source in aquatic communities. Leopard Frogs feed voraciously on all manner of insect life.

African Bullfrog *Pyxicephalus adspersus*

Although hardly descriptive of them, these frogs are known to many as "Pyxies." With adult males reaching nine inches in some parts of its range, this burly amphibian has a broad, rounded head, horizontal pupils, and webbed toes. It bears a flange-like structure along the inner edge of the foot to aid in digging. Easily the largest amphibian in Central Africa, the "Pyxie" ranges from Nigeria to Somalia southward to South Africa excluding the southwestern Cape Province. Spending as much as ten months of the year underground, Pyxies emerge at the onset of seasonal rains to congregate around pools of water where they breed. As many as 1200 eggs may be produced by one female; these are deposited into the water. Tadpoles are guarded against other predators, although the brooding female herself may consume some of her offspring. This presumably provides energy, allowing her to continue the task at hand.

The photo above shows how large this species can become. This frog has puffed itself up as a defensive measure. It tries to avoid being eaten by making itself too large for a snake to swallow.

The African Bullfrog on the left has a juvenile on its head. This pose is not usually seen in nature because the parent would be likely to eat its offspring.

Musky Flying Frog
Rhacophorus reinwardtii

A complex of species native to Java, Sumatra, the Malay Peninsula, and portions of adjacent China, this is one of the most familiar species of flying frog. Living in primary and secondary lowland rainforest, bamboo groves, and thickets, the Musky Flying Frog possesses extensive dermal flaps and massively webbed hands and feet so that it is able to glide from tree to tree. The three-and-one-half-inch females deposit their eggs in foam nests high in the trees.

Madagascan Lined Frog
Heterixalus rutenbergi

One of Madagascar's most uniquely colored amphibians, this one-inch species is found in the east-central part of the country. Preferred habitat appears to be open marshy grassland and swamps with sunny exposures. Little is known about this frog.

Cashew Frog *Nyctimantis rugiceps*

This three-inch treefrog, although large and gaudy, is one of the least known Amazonian amphibians. A tree-hole dweller long known only from Ecuador, the specimen above was photographed in Peru, and this frog probably also occurs in Colombia. It is hard to locate because it lives high in the trees. When startled, it retreats into its water-filled lair. If handled, it exudes a toxic skin secretion which smells like the fruit of the Cashew Tree. Its diet consists of insects.

Jewel Treefrog *Hyla miyatai* (photo at right)

This one-inch frog was only discovered and described within the last decade. It lives in the Upper Amazon Basin of Colombia, Ecuador, Peru, and probably Brazil.

Gladiator Treefrog *Hyla boans* (photo at left)

When the dry season lowers the river levels in Panama and northern South America, this five-inch treefrog climbs down from the trees and excavates distinctive, round depressions in the sand by the water. Females lay their eggs in these pools and the tadpoles hatch in the calm waters. Gladiator Treefrogs are so named because the males engage in combat during the breeding season. Their diet consists of insects.

Painted Mantella
Mantella madagascariensis

This frog is a denizen of Madagascar's eastern rainforests. The males call intensely during the day from hiding places on the ground along fast-flowing streams.

Introduction to Mantellas
Mantella sp.

These are the most distinctive of the Madagascan frogs. There are about 13 frogs in this genus; all are small, lack webbing on the hands and feet, and most sport beautiful colors and patterns. At a glance, most are strongly reminiscent of the Poison Frogs found in Central and South America. Indeed, they have similar habitats, favoring moist rainforests, some have toxins in the skin, and some species will climb and breed in tree holes. Averaging less than one and one-half inches in length, Mantellas are active by day, feeding mostly on small insects like ants and termites. Small, jelly-covered patches of 12 to 24 eggs are laid on the ground. Due to their relatively slow rate of reproduction and to habitat destruction, some Mantella species are declining in numbers.

Golden Mantella *Mantella aurantiaca*

Golden Mantella (red phase) *Mantella aurantiaca*

GS

Masked Mantella
Mantella viridis

This attractive frog, which can exceed one inch in size, is restricted to the northern tip of Madagascar. The Masked Mantella is a forest dweller, usually found in close proximity to streams or other wet areas. Interestingly, aggression has been noted between captive females of this species, although the reason is unknown. The diet of the Masked Mantella consists of small insects.

GS

Painted Mantella
Mantella madagascariensis

Beautiful Mantella *Mantella pulchra*

The natural history of this inhabitant of Madagascar's humid eastern rainforests is unknown. Some populations are blue, while others are green or grayish. Males call during the day.

Pigmy Mantella *Mantella bernhardi*

Also known as Bernhard's Mantella, this frog was described only recently and is still known from only one locality in eastern Madagascar. Males of this tiny frog have been observed to call by day from exposed locations on the forest floor. The largest specimens known measure less than one inch in length.

Masked Mantella *Mantella viridis*

Sonoran Green Toad *Bufo retiformis*

Adapted to dry regions in Arizona and adjacent Sonora, Mexico, these two-inch toads are seldom seen above ground. Summer rains cause them to congregate in puddles for breeding, and the tadpoles develop quickly before their water evaporates. Highways and other habitat destruction have taken their toll, and the Green Toad is now protected by law.

Chilean Toad

Bufo variegatus

Few of the world's toads can be described as colorful, most tending towards somber attire. But this little two-inch species is the exception. Native to cold Andean forests from southern Peru to Patagonia, Argentina, and southern Chile, this toad reaches nearly the southernmost point attained by amphibians. A clumsy jumper and poor swimmer, the Chilean Toad spends much of its time sheltered in ground mosses. Small ponds serve as breeding sites, and insects make up its diet.

Malaysian Leaf Frog

Megophrys nasuta

Some leaf mimics feature countershading in their color pattern. Their sides are notably darker than their backs, and this serves to disrupt the outline of the animal, further confusing both predators and prey. Malaysian Leaf Frogs also bear distinctive triangular flaps of skin over their eyes. Sitting motionless among the leaves on the forest floor, they are practically undetectable. This four-inch amphibian ranges from Thailand southeast to Sumatra and Borneo.

Spotted Tree Toad *Pedostibes hosii*

This strange, long-limbed amphibian is native to Borneo, Sumatra, Malaya, and extreme southern Thailand. Females, much larger and more colorfully marked than males, may attain five inches in length. A forest species, the Spotted Tree Toad feeds primarily upon ants. Males call at night from low shrubbery along streams. Eggs are deposited in the water.

The photo, at left, of the Malaysian Leaf Frog, indicates how perfectly its camouflage colors blend with its leafy habitat. It also illustrates how this frog's back is much paler in color than its underside, an example of countershading.

Cayenne Harlequin Toad *Atelopus flavescens*

This species is found in northeastern South America in French Guiana and adjacent Brazil. Maximum length is under two inches. The Cayenne Harlequin Toad lives in lowland coastal rain forests, where it hunts on the forest floor for small insects.

Introduction to Harlequin Toads *Atelopus sp.*

These small toads include more than 66 species that live in tropical or subtropical regions from Costa Rica to Bolivia. Generally slow-moving and often brightly colored, these attractive amphibians are often confused with Poison Frogs (*Dendrobates* and related genera). Indeed, *Atelopus* may be found to possess toxic skin secretions like the dendrobatids. Harlequin Toads feed on tiny insects, including ants and termites. Several species of harlequin toads exhibit considerable variation in color and pattern, and some of these may prove to contain additional species when they are studied. Most *Atelopus* are diurnal, terrestrial, rather bold, and are often found walking near streams. However, the Panama Golden Toad, *Atelopus zeteki*, is shy and nocturnal. Some species are "explosive breeders," with several dozen males surrounding a single female. Eggs are deposited in small jellied strings in streams. Most species are no more than one inch in length as adults.

Variable Harlequin Toad
Atelopus varius

This two-and-one-half-inch amphibian makes its home in lowland and lower montane rainforests in Costa Rica and Panama. As its name implies, it varies in color and pattern, actually appearing more like a group of species rather than one.

Panama Golden Toad *Atelopus zeteki*

Its startling yellow or orange color lends an exotic air to this two-and-one-half-inch amphibian. Native to Panama, where it is known to inhabit Pacific lowland forest in just two provinces, its numbers appear to be dwindling. Most members of the genus *Atelopus* are slow, terrestrial walkers. They are usually found along forested streams. However, the Panama Golden Toad has been found as high as 12 feet above ground.

Peruvian Harlequin Toad

Atelopus peruensis (below)

This robust, two-inch toad lives in the high Andes of the Peruvian department of Cajamarca. It is active by day in bunch grass and puna, a high-Andean zone characterized by dry, open regions and cold temperatures.

Amazon Harlequin Toad

Atelopus pulcher pulcher (above)

Some Harlequin Toads, when threatened, arch their back while raising and exposing their palms and soles, which are red. This maneuver, called an *"unken reflex,"* warns predators of the toxic nature of the toad's skin. The Amazon Harlequin Toad ranges throughout the lowlands of the Amazon Basin in South America.

Red-handed Walking Toad
Melanophryniscus stelzneri stelzneri

Living at intermediate elevations in two Argentinian mountain ranges, this one-and-one-half-inch frog can be found along stream beds after summer rains. It's call, given in the early morning, emanates from grassy clumps which serve as hideouts. When threatened, this amphibian arches its back and curls its red palms and soles upward, creating a startling display to ward off predators. Slow and clumsy, the Red-handed Walking Toad is inept at jumping and swimming. Food consists primarily of ants and aphids.

Amazon Moustache Frog
Leptodactylus rhodomystax

This stocky, five-inch frog is a powerful digger, excavating a burrow in the leaf litter of the rain forest floor of its native Amazon Basin. During warm, rainy nights the Moustache Frog sits at the entrance of its burrow and calls, retreating at the slightest warning. These frogs construct foam nests in the leaf litter, thus keeping their eggs moist in the absence of water. Their diet consists of insects.

Golden Toad *Bufo periglenes*

Most frogs and toads breed at night, so it is uncommon to encounter a species exhibiting sexual color differences. Such is not the case with the Golden Toad. Mating occurs during the day in the dim surroundings of the cloud forest floor of its native Costa Rica. Male Golden Toads are startlingly brilliant yellow-orange, while the larger females are olive with bold red spots. Presumably these colors play an important role for this species.

This photo shows a pair of Golden Toads spawning. The male fertilizes the eggs as they are laid by the female. Tadpoles will emerge and complete their development in the water.

The Golden Toad at left is an example of an unusually dark specimen. The normal color is a bright pumpkin orange.

The Golden Toad has become important for a very unfortunate reason: it may be extinct. Not a single specimen has been seen for a number of years in spite of intensive efforts to locate them. Scientists are pondering the reasons for the tragic disappearance of this and many other frogs and toads around the world, and the Golden Toad has become an international symbol of the alarming decline of amphibians.

Fire-bellied Toad *Bombina orientalis*

Diminutive pond-dwellers, ranging from the Soviet Far East through northeast China to Korea, these toads blend nicely with their surroundings. However, should camouflage fail, the startling effect of the brilliant underside might cause potential predators to hesitate, allowing the toad critical time for escape. Hardy insect feeders, Fire-bellied Toads have long been the subject of genetic research due to the ease with which they can be bred and maintained in the laboratory.

Suriname Toad

Pipa pipa

The flattened body, broad head, and pig-like eyes make this one of the world's most bizarre amphibians. Long the object of laboratory investigations, this strange frog is also a staple item in the aquarium industry. Completely aquatic (although they do occasionally climb onto the banks at the edges of ponds or streams), Suriname Toads feed primarily on minnows, which they inhale with great speed. After fertilizing the eggs, male Suriname Toads press them onto the female's back, where they soon sink in. The resulting "honeycomb" houses the eggs until fully-formed froglets emerge and swim away. Suriname Toads are native to the Orinoco and Amazon Basins of South America. Their maximum size is about seven inches.

This photo shows Rain Frog (*Eleutherodactylus sp.*) froglets developing inside the egg. This is a case of "direct development." The tadpole stage is skipped. Worldwide, there are many species of frogs which undergo direct development.

This is a Cat-eyed Snake (*Leptodeira*) swallowing the eggs of a Red-eyed Leaf Frog. Frogs, their eggs, and larvae are favorite prey items of many snake species.

Two male Glass Frogs (*Hyalinobatrachium valerioi*), each abandoned by its female partner, guard their broods of eggs. Later, the tadpoles will fall into a stream below.

The Photographers: Pete Carmichael and Gail Shumway

For over three decades, Pete Carmichael's photographs have delighted nature-lovers. Pete is best known for his seashell, butterfly, and rainforest photography. He is the photographer for the acclaimed *World's Most Beautiful Seashells* (winner of the Coffee Table Book Award of the National Association of Independent Publishers), and the very popular *Florida's Fabulous Reptiles and Amphibians*. He is frequently featured in national and international nature magazines.

Gail Shumway's work has appeared on covers of *National Wildlife, International Wildlife* and *Ranger Rick* magazines. In 1986 she was the Grand Prize winner of the International Wildlife Photography Contest, and she also won national awards in 1987 and 1988. In 1997 she received the Distinguished Achievement Award of the Educational Press Association of America for excellence in educational journalism. Her other credits include *Florida Wildlife Magazine, Birder's World, Audubon, Sierra Club, World Wildlife Fund,* and *Smithsonian*.

The Author: William W. Lamar

Bill Lamar has spent over half his life investigating reptiles and amphibians in the remote rainforests of Central and South America. After residing for many years in Colombia, Lamar worked in ten other countries. Author of numerous scientific and popular articles, he also co-authored the monumental book, THE VENOMOUS REPTILES OF LATIN AMERICA, considered a modern classic in the field of herpetology. Lamar's wildlife photographs are widely known and have graced the covers of numerous books and magazines.

Lamar is Adjunct Professor of Biology at the University of Texas at Tyler; Research Associate of the Collection of Vertebrates at the University of Texas, Arlington; Associate Herpetologist at the University of Kansas Museum of Natural History; and Associate Herpetologist at the National Serpentarium in San José, Costa Rica. He has been featured in films made by the BBC, National Geographic Explorer, the Canadian Broadcasting Company, and NOVA.

Along with colleagues George Gorman and George Ledvina, Lamar founded Green Tracks, Inc., a Tyler, Texas-based eco-tour company providing general and specialized trips worldwide for those interested in tropical wildlife. He can now be reached through the Green Tracks offices at 903-593-7170 or 800-966-6539, or on the web at Greentracks.com.

Contributing Author: William B. Love

Bill Love, a well-known columnist in popular herpetological magazines, provided a number of species accounts for an earlier version of this book. Some of this material remains in the current version. Bill and his wife, Kathy, are familiar to many in the herpetological movement. Together, they toured the country with a popular educational exhibit on reptiles and amphibians. Bill and Kathy's new business enterprise, Blue Chameleon Ventures, is based in Alva, Florida. Bill is widely recognized for his outstanding photography, and a number of his photos appear in this book.